Sony Vegas Pro 11 Beginner's Guide

Edit videos with style and ease using Vegas Pro

Duncan Wood

BIRMINGHAM - MUMBAI

Sony Vegas Pro 11 Beginner's Guide

First published: July 2012

Production Reference: 1200712

Published by Packt Publishing Ltd.
Livery Place
35 Livery Street
Birmingham B3 2PB, UK.

ISBN 978-1-84969-170-3

www.packtpub.com

Cover Image by Faiz Fattohi (faizfattohi@gmail.com)

Credits

Author

Duncan Wood

Reviewers

Chris Bryant

Einar Ritsmer

Jeff Schroeder

Cooper Rory

Acquisition Editor

Wilson D'souza

Lead Technical Editor

Arun Nadar

Technical Editors

Apoorva Bolar

Conrad Neil Sardinha

Project Coordinator

Leena Purkait

Proofreader

Matthew Humphries

Indexer

Hemangini Bari

Production Coordinator

Nilesh R. Mohite

Cover Work

Nilesh R. Mohite

About the Author

A 35 year veteran of the music and video industries, **Duncan Wood** has certainly seen his share of changes and advances in technologies in these two fields. Having worked with a large range of music artists from household names, such as, Savage Garden, The Veronicas, and Jon English, through to a list way too long to mention of unknown and up and comers, Duncan has had hands on experience starting in the days of analogue tape and video through to today's digital media formats. As owner and director of his company Touchwood Productions (www.touchwoodproductions.com), Duncan is active on a daily basis pushing the boundaries and forging pathways to have his productions see light of day in this ever changing landscape of the multimedia industries.

Always keen to help the next generation of music and video editors strive to succeed, Duncan has been excited to write the *Beginners Guide* for *Sony Vegas Pro 11*. His hands on experience combined with his years of experience presented in the Packt Publishing book format will make for an exciting read for those keen to conquer this powerful software.

I would like to thank my wonderful wife Caroline Taylor-Knight for her support and encouragement in all I do, as well as Sienna Susan Wood, my 20 month old daughter (at the writing of this bio) for the amazing things that she has taught me about life, love, and family. I would also like to thank Leena Purkait and Wilson D'souza from Packt Publishing for their guidance and assistance throughout the process of writing this book.

I also want to thank the artist Dane Sharp who appears in the footage for the Music Video tutorial and is the singer of the song One Way Ride.

About the Reviewers

After standing in line for hours to watch Jurassic Park on the opening night, **Chris Bryant** was instantly hooked on motion pictures. He also realized at an early age that if you don't want to be filmed, you needed to be the one holding the camera! One of his first paychecks went to purchase an 8 mm camcorder, and his passion for video production has grown ever since. He edited his first video back in high school by chaining together two VCRs to create a thematic introduction to his senior project, and was a Media Arts major at Western Connecticut State University.

He eventually went on to start his own company in 2004 (look for Bryant Productions on Facebook!) and films a range of promotional and internal training videos for companies nationwide.

For fun he produces short films including *The Other Half*, the first place winner of the 2009 Connecticut Film Festival's *24 Hour Cup 'O Joe Filmmaking Competition*. Chris has experience as a voiceover artist and event videographer.

When he isn't shooting video or editing, Chris enjoys spending time with his beautiful wife and three dogs at their home in Connecticut.

Einar Ritsmer is an enthusiastic videographer recording and editing several videos every year. He has a M.Sc. in electrical engineering and IT. Einar participates in various peer-to-peer video forums giving advice on video editing and editing hardware. He is also a **Sony Certified Vegas User (SCVU)**.

www.PacktPub.com

Support files, eBooks, discount offers and more

You might want to visit www.PacktPub.com for support files and downloads related to your book.

Did you know that Packt offers eBook versions of every book published, with PDF and ePub files available? You can upgrade to the eBook version at www.PacktPub.com and as a print book customer, you are entitled to a discount on the eBook copy. Get in touch with us at service@packtpub.com for more details.

At www.PacktPub.com, you can also read a collection of free technical articles, sign up for a range of free newsletters, and receive exclusive discounts and offers on Packt books and eBooks.

 PACKTLiB®

http://PacktLib.PacktPub.com

Do you need instant solutions to your IT questions? PacktLib is Packt's online digital book library. Here, you can access, read, and search across Packt's entire library of books.

Why Subscribe?

- ◆ Fully searchable across every book published by Packt
- ◆ Copy and paste, print, and bookmark content
- ◆ On demand and accessible via web browsers

Free Access for Packt account holders

If you have an account with Packt at www.PacktPub.com, you can use this to access PacktLib today and view nine entirely free books. Simply use your login credentials for immediate access.

Table of Contents

Preface

The Beginner's Guide to Sony Vegas Pro 11 is a great education and revision tool for the users of this powerful video editing software package. By working through the tutorial projects, the reader will gain a strong understanding of how the software works and the processes for creating exciting video projects. For the experienced user, this book will help to revise their editing workflow as well as show alternate and possibly more efficient ways of achieving professional results.

What this book covers

Chapter 1, Getting Acquainted with your New Best Friend: Vegas Pro 11 Overview, covers system requirements to run the discussed software and the process of installing Sony Vegas Pro 11. This is followed by an introduction to the user interface and its associated windows plus an overview of the *Tutorial Project* we will be using with this book.

Chapter 2, Let the Magic Begin: Beginning the Project and Acquiring Media, explains some of the most important topics for getting started with Vegas Pro 11. They include, *How to create a Project, Pixel Aspect Ratio, The Preview Monitor, Importing of Media, The Smart Tool*, and *Keyboard Shortcuts*.

Chapter 3, Video Editing Concepts and Application, discusses the history of film making and editing as well as information on what makes a good edit. We look at the multi-camera tool which will be used in our tutorial, plus essential functions for editing, such as panning and cropping and slow and fast motion video.

Chapter 4, Essential Editing Tools, discusses the tools and their workflows as well as gives some insight into the software's 3D editing capabilities.

Chapter 5, Eye Catching Titles, Text, and Effects, discusses the tools that go a long way in helping the reader bring their video editing workflows into the professional league.

Chapter 6, Color Correction Techniques, shows the reader how to use the all important color correction tools to their best advantage.

Chapter 7, Look, I Made it Move!!—Automating Tools in Sony Vegas, dives into one of the biggest advantages of digital non-linear video editing, which is the ability to automate or animate most, if not all of the tools in Sony Vegas Pro 11.

Chapter 8, The Importance of Audio, discusses the importance of audio for vision and the tools used to create that experience.

Chapter 9, Soundtrack of our Lives: Audio for Video, discusses creating great audio including the spoken word and microphones, as well as music copyright, ways to create original music for your projects, and the concepts of surround sound audio.

Chapter 10, Can I put this on YouTube?: Rendering and Delivering the Final Project, helps the reader to negotiate the often scary path through video compression and codecs, video and audio formats, and confidently choosing the right formats for creating the final delivery method whether it be DVD, Blu-ray via DVD Architect, or the Internet.

What you need for this book

To successfully use this book, the most current version of Sony Vegas Pro 11 is needed and installed onto your video editing computer system. Although there may be a few small interface differences, this book will also be useful for users of the latest version of Sony Vegas Pro 10. You will also need to download the video and audio files for the project that you will be working on during the tutorials in this book.

Who this book is for

The Beginner's Guide to Sony Vegas Pro 11, although ideally suited to the video editing newcomer, will also appeal to both professional and intermediate users looking for helpful and insightful ways of carrying out tasks in their video editing workflow.

Conventions

In this book you will find a number of styles of text that distinguish between different kinds of information. Here are some examples of these styles, and an explanation of their meaning.

New terms and **important words** are shown in bold. Words that you see on the screen, in menus or dialog boxes for example, appear in the text like this: "You can check if you have the latest version by selecting **HELP MENU | Sony on the Web | Latest Updates**".

Warnings or important notes appear in a box like this.

Although not essential, I would highly recommend having a second hard drive to store and edit your video project's media. This drive should also be at least a 7200 RPM drive as this will free up the system drive and be less taxing on the overall system.

Reader feedback

Feedback from our readers is always welcome. Let us know what you think about this book—what you liked or may have disliked. Reader feedback is important for us to develop titles that you really get the most out of.

To send us general feedback, simply send an e-mail to feedback@packtpub.com, and mention the book title through the subject of your message.

If there is a topic that you have expertise in and you are interested in either writing or contributing to a book, see our author guide on www.packtpub.com/authors.

Customer support

Now that you are the proud owner of a Packt book, we have a number of things to help you to get the most from your purchase.

Downloading the example code

You can download the example code files for all Packt books you have purchased from your account at http://www.packtpub.com. If you purchased this book elsewhere, you can visit http://www.packtpub.com/support and register to have the files e-mailed directly to you.

Errata

Although we have taken every care to ensure the accuracy of our content, mistakes do happen. If you find a mistake in one of our books—maybe a mistake in the text or the code—we would be grateful if you would report this to us. By doing so, you can save other readers from frustration and help us improve subsequent versions of this book. If you find any errata, please report them by visiting http://www.packtpub.com/support, selecting your book, clicking on the **errata submission form** link, and entering the details of your errata. Once your errata are verified, your submission will be accepted and the errata will be uploaded to our website, or added to any list of existing errata, under the Errata section of that title.

Piracy

Piracy of copyright material on the Internet is an ongoing problem across all media. At Packt, we take the protection of our copyright and licenses very seriously. If you come across any illegal copies of our works, in any form, on the Internet, please provide us with the location address or website name immediately so that we can pursue a remedy.

Please contact us at copyright@packtpub.com with a link to the suspected pirated material.

We appreciate your help in protecting our authors, and our ability to bring you valuable content.

Questions

You can contact us at questions@packtpub.com if you are having a problem with any aspect of the book, and we will do our best to address it.

1

Getting Acquainted with your New Best Friend: Vegas Pro 11 Overview

Every piece of software we utilize in our creative world seems to become one of our best friends, especially if it is our main go-to application for a specific task. We communicate with it every day and sometimes spend many hours interfacing with it. So the day comes when that software and you decide to take the relationship to a new level and it moves in with you, and takes up permanent residence on your PC. Just like a new housemate, we want to make sure it has all of the modern conveniences and space it needs to give you both a carefree coexistence.

So let's move him / her in...

In this chapter, we shall cover:

- System requirements
- Exploring the Vegas Pro windows
- Customizing the User Interface
- Overview of Vegas Project we will be working with

A note on your computer

A video editor's computer system will vary from user to user. With this in mind, Sony has made the Vegas Pro 11 software to be quite forgiving of any inefficiency that your system may have. So to ensure a happy first project, please ensure you have installed the latest version and build of Vegas Pro 11. You can check if you have the latest version by selecting **Help | Sony on the Web | Latest Updates** from the menu bar.

System requirements

Included on your installation disks or bundled with your downloaded installation file from Sony Creative Software Inc., is a list of **Minimum System Requirements** needed to successfully run Vegas Pro 11.

In order to use this book and the downloaded project, your system must satisfy those requirements.

Please refer to your Sony Vegas Pro 11 user manual for more details on this topic.

If you purchased Vegas Pro 11 online you can download the manual from `http://www.sonycreativesoftware.com/download/manuals/vegaspro`.

Also technical support, reference information, program updates, tips and tricks, a user's forum, and a knowledge base are available from `http://www.sonycreativesoftware.com/support/default.asp`.

Although not essential, I would highly recommend having a second hard drive to store and edit your video project's media. This drive should also be at least a 7200 RPM drive as this will free up the system drive and be less taxing on the overall system.

Getting help

Vegas Pro 11 also comes with two varieties of help available to you. Besides this beginners' guide you can access powerful information via:

- Online Help
- Interactive Tutorials

Online Help

Online help is accessible once Vegas Pro 11 is running on your computer by choosing **Contents and Index** from the **Help** menu or by pressing F1.

You can also access more help and information via the Sony Creative Software Inc website by choosing **Sony on the Web** from the **Help** menu.

[Tip: Please note that your computer must be connected to the Internet for the **Sony on the Web** function to operate.]

Interactive Tutorials

You can also learn more about the many features in Vegas Pro 11 by accessing the interactive tutorials installed with the software. The tutorials will be displayed once you start the software, but you can also access them from the **Help** menu listed as **Interactive Tutorials**.

[Tip: The automatic display of tutorials can be turned off by un-checking the **Show at Start-up box** at the bottom of the tutorial window.]

Getting to know the windows: Exploring the Vegas Pro 11 interface

Communication is the key to any relationship, and the same applies with your newly-installed software. Knowing how and where to access the right tools while editing is crucial, and will allow you to easily interact with Vegas Pro 11. The Graphical User Interface or GUI in Vegas Pro 11 is fairly complex, with many windows that contain all of the important tools for editing your video. Here we will overview each of these user interface elements to get you more acquainted with the windows of Vegas Pro 11, before we plunge into their uses in our Beginner's Guide Project.

The Vegas Pro 11 windows

The Sony Vegas Pro 11 user interface has many windows with which to access the tools and functions of the software, so let's go through each of the important windows to familiarize ourselves with them before we start the actual editing process:

- **The Track Header**

  The next screenshot shows you the **Track Header**. Here Vegas Pro Projects display Video, Audio, Video Bus, and Audio Bus tracks in the list for your Project. Extending to the right into the **Timeline**, the tracks allow you to arrange your audio, video, Still Images, Backgrounds, and Text. All of the settings for the tracks can be found here including volume and panning, Video Compositing Level, applying temporary Solo and Muting to both video and audio, apply Track motion, changing the Recording Mode, or changing the Track Height. If you hover your mouse over any of the buttons and icons, its name will appear for you:

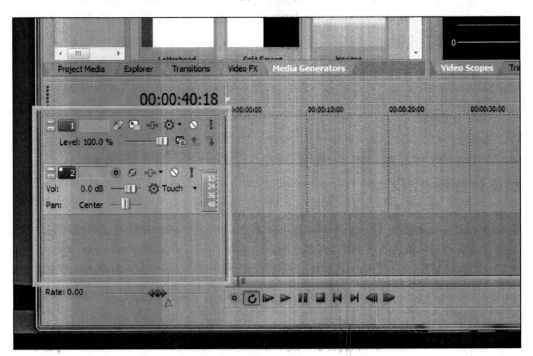

◆ The Timeline

The Timeline is your main work area, which allows you to arrange and edit all of your audio, video, and still images to create your final project movie. Horizontally reading from left to right, the timeline represents *time*.

Think of a film strip or unraveled audio tape laid out on the timeline where you can see what you are editing. Vertically the timeline shows **Tracks**. Tracks are where you place your audio or video files and are known as **Events**. The timeline allows you to precisely control the length and time placements of your events:

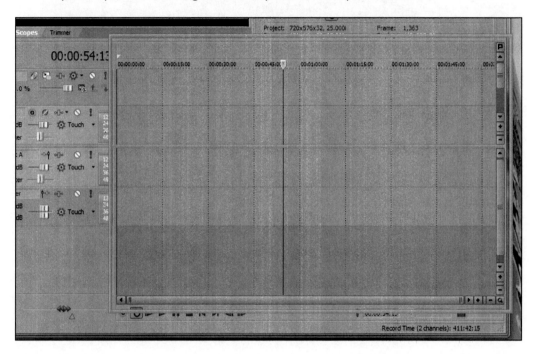

- **The Transport toolbar**

  The Transport toolbar allows you to control the playback of your project just like a tape deck or CD player. Clicking the play button will allow you to watch your video update in the Video Preview window. As with most tools in Vegas, there are multiple ways to utilize them. The **Play** and **Stop** buttons can also be accessed by pressing the *Space bar* to alternate between the play and stop functions of your video:

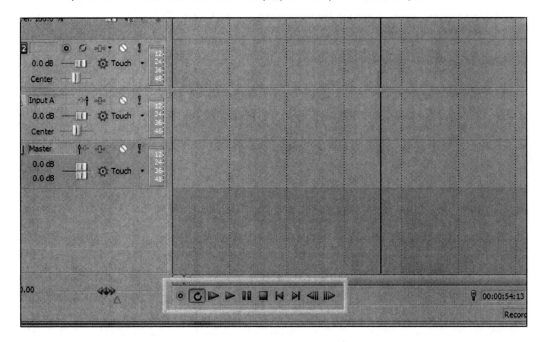

- ◆ **The Time Display**

  The Vegas Pro Time Display shows the current position of the cursor on the timeline. This display uses the industry standard format of HH:MM:SS: FF where HH is Hours, MM is Minutes, SS is Seconds, and FF is the current video frame the cursor is on within that second. For example, the following screenshot indicates the cursor is sitting on the 12th second of the timeline and on the 19th frame of that second. If the **Project Settings** were set to a **PAL Video**, that would be the 19th Frame out of the 25 frames allocated for that second:

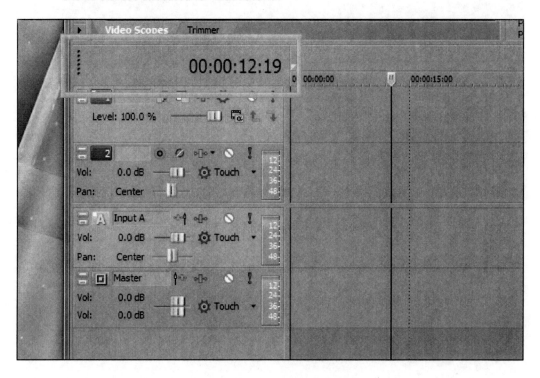

◆ **The Status bar**

The Status bar of the timeline shows us three numeric boxes which represent the highlighted selection's **Starting Time**, **Ending Time**, and **Duration**. If there is no selection, the first box displays the **Cursor Position** only:

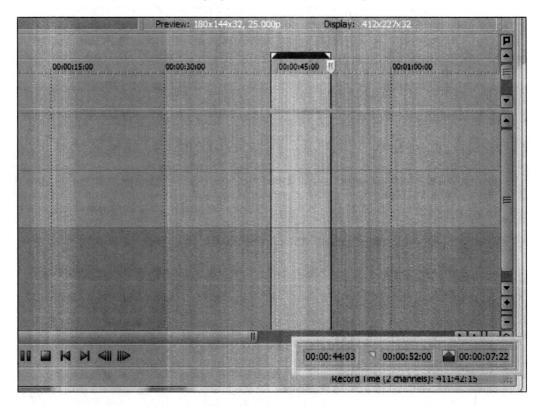

◆ **The Explorer window**

By clicking on the **Explorer** tab just above the time display, or using key combination *ALT + 1*, the **Explorer** window is available. Here, you can quickly browse your entire computer and connected hard drives and network places for audio, video, and still images for your project. You can *click*-and-*drag* the files from the Explorer window into the timeline to make them available for use in your project. Once a file is dragged into the timeline, it automatically becomes available in the Project Media window:

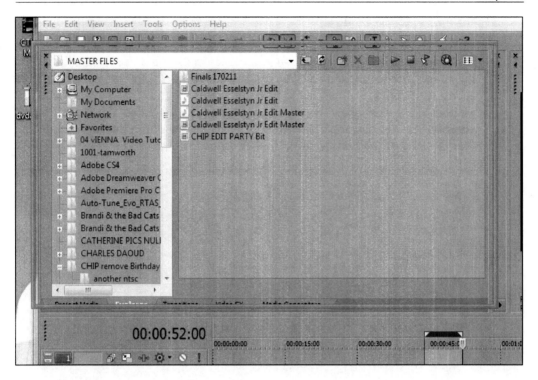

- **XDCAM Explorer**

    The **XDCAM Explorer** window can be accessed by using *CTRL + ALT + 5*. XDCAM files can be efficiently handled by this window so you can select and preview the files before dropping them onto the timeline for editing:

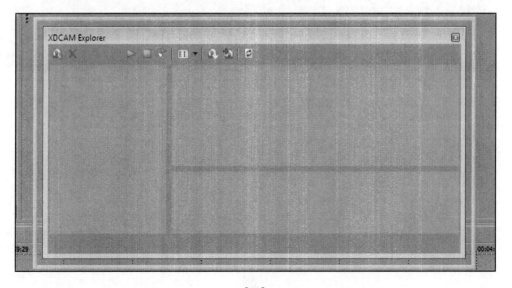

◆ **The Project Media window**

Click on the **Project Media** tab or use *ALT + 5*. The **Project Media** window shows you all of the media being currently used in your project. Media consists of audio, video, still images, backdrops, and text. You can also add media to your project by using the appropriate icon buttons which can be found across the top of the Project Media window. These icons allow you to: **Import Media, Capture Video, Get Photo from attached Scanner, Extract Audio from CD**, and **Get Media from the Web**. Hover your mouse over the icons to reveal their function.

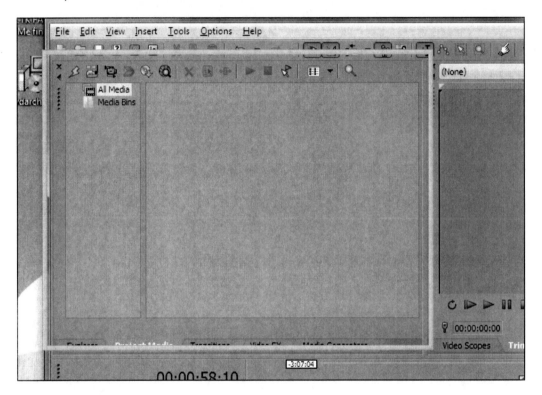

◆ **The Trimmer**

Select the **Trimmer** tab or use *ALT + 2*. The **Trimmer** window is another useful editing tool at your disposal. In the trimmer, a portion of a media clip can be selected or trimmed and inserted into your project. You also have the ability to create subclips in the **Trimmer** window. A subclip allows you to leave the original media fully intact while creating a new shorter clip extracted from the original:

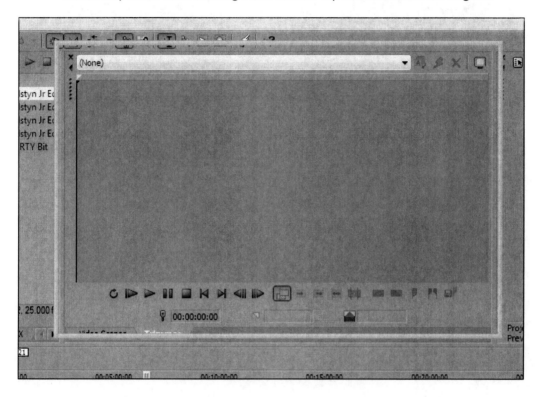

◆ **The Mixer window**

Select the **Mixer** window by using *ALT + 3*. The **Mixer** window in Vegas Pro 11 is a very powerful audio tool that allows for complete Final Mixing and Processing of your project's audio and soundtrack:

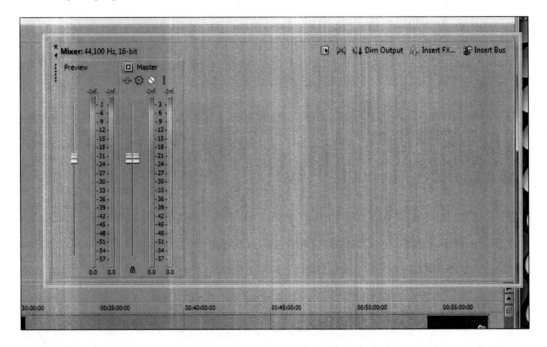

- **Mixing Console**

  The **Mixing Console** window is a full featured traditional audio mixing console. It contains many of the same features as the Track Header, but is laid out in a recognizable and expected Audio Console format. The complexities and fun of audio mixing will be covered in *Chapter 7, Look, I Made it Move!! : Automating Tools in Sony Vegas* and *Chapter 8, The Importance of Audio*.

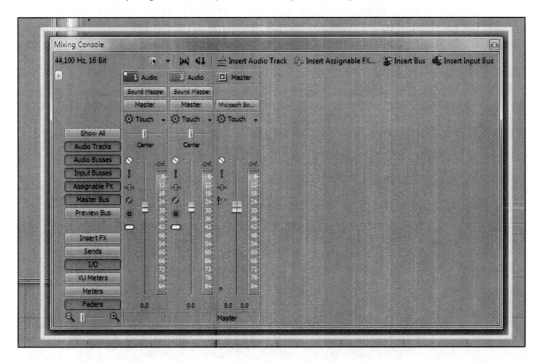

◆ **The Video Preview** window

Press *ALT + 4* to bring up the **Video Preview** window. This preview generally displays the video output from your selected point on the timeline. The smoothness, quality, and clarity of the **preview** window depends greatly on the fine balance between the processing power available from your CPU and video card, the number and type of FX plugins you have on your media, and the preview quality setting you have chosen. The Preview Quality settings range from **Draft**, **Preview**, **Good**, and **Best**, but generally **Preview Auto** will be sufficient. One of the big pluses of Vegas Pro 11 is that it will now utilize the GPU processor on your video card as long as your video card supports the OpenCL architecture.

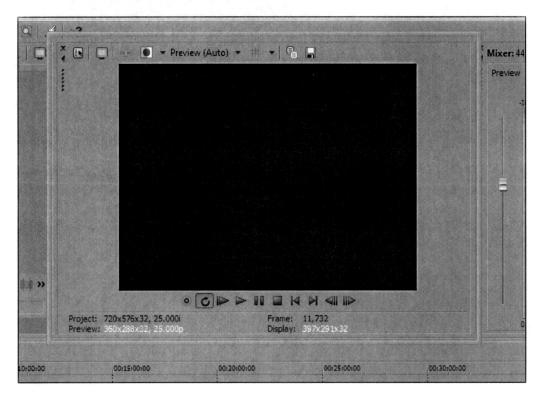

◆ **Transitions window**

Select the **Transitions** tab or *ALT + 7* to open the **Transitions** window. Transitions are used to smoothly connect one media clip to another. Transitions sometimes can represent things such as time passing, travelling from interior to exterior, or from one scene to another. They are itemized by category in the left column with an animated representation of how the transition works on the right. The transitions can be quickly applied to two overlapping media clips by clicking-and-dragging the transition into the cross-faded media clips to add or change the transition:

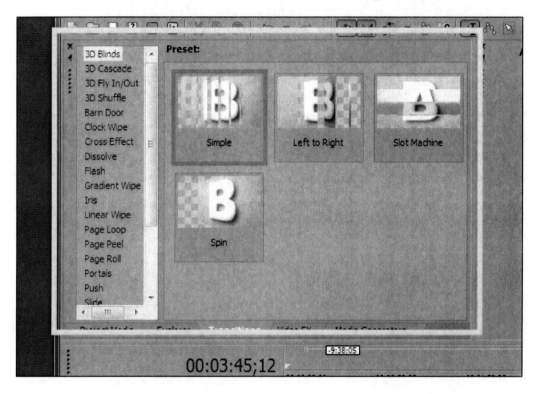

◆ **Video FX**

Select the **Video FX** tab or use *ALT + 8* to open the **Video FX** window. Like the Transitions window, the selection of **Video FX** that can be applied to your video clips are itemized into categories on the left with an appropriate animation on the right to give you an idea of what the FX does. **Video FX** range from creative choices, such as Blurs and Color FX, through to corrective FX such as Brightness, Contrast, and Sharpness with a myriad of choices in between. You can click-and-drag the FX onto your media clips and you can also apply multiple FX on top of each other onto a single clip. Once in place the presets can be animated over time:

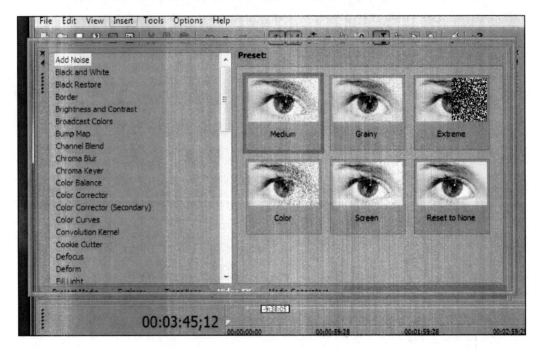

◆ **Media Generators**

The **Media Generator** window can be accessed by selecting the **Media Generator** tab or using *ALT + 9*. This window will access many backdrop FX, color gradients, checkerboards, and some very powerful text and pro type titler generators. Dragging the selected preset onto the timeline will allow you to change the properties to suit your project as well as animate the generated media for truly stunning effects.

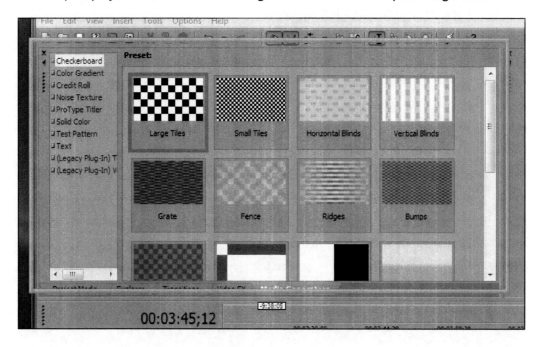

◆ **Device Explorer**

Using *CTRL + ALT + 7* will open the **Device Explorer** window. With the advent of many different format cameras available, Vegas Pro 11 can now communicate directly with these camera devices to import their clips into your project. The Device Explorer will search for any such devices and allow you to browse the files and import them. Formats such as AVCHD, XDCAM XE, and RED ONE cameras will all communicate happily via this window.

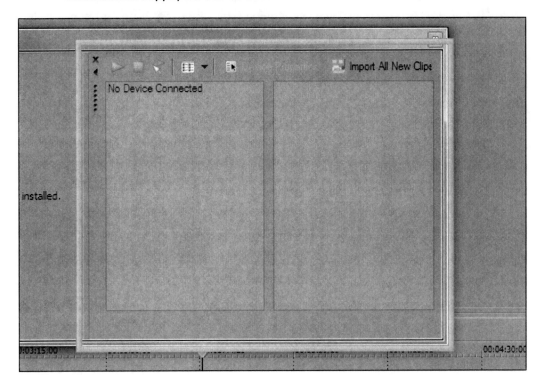

◆ **Video Scopes window**

The **Video Scopes** window is accessed by using *CTRL + ALT + 2*. These Scopes and Histograms allow for accurate analyzing of the color and white balance of your video playback. They will become a very useful tool for the trained eye.

Customizing the User Interface

As we have seen in the previous section, there are many windows to access the tools and functions we will need while editing. Another great feature of Vegas Pro 11 is the ability to setup and display these windows in a way that suits your own personal taste and way of working. Let's learn how to make a custom window layout.

Time for action – customizing the Vegas User Interface

1. With a Blank Vegas Project open, select *ALT + 4* to make sure your Preview window is open. You will notice a vertical row of six dots circled, in the top-left corner of the Preview window, as shown in the following screenshot:

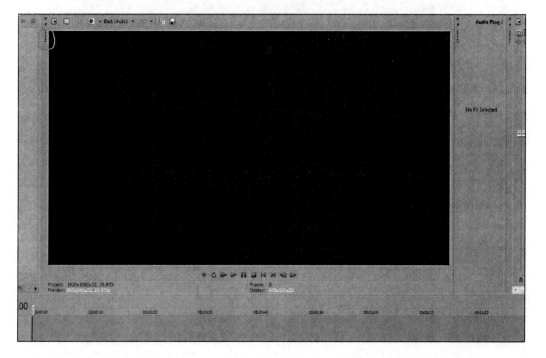

2. These dots create a handle with which to grab and move the window either on to another part of the window dock or to a completely different position on the screen independent of the Vegas User Interface. Click-and-hold the row of dots and drag the Preview window so that it becomes independent of the other windows and floats on top of the interface, as shown in the following screenshot:

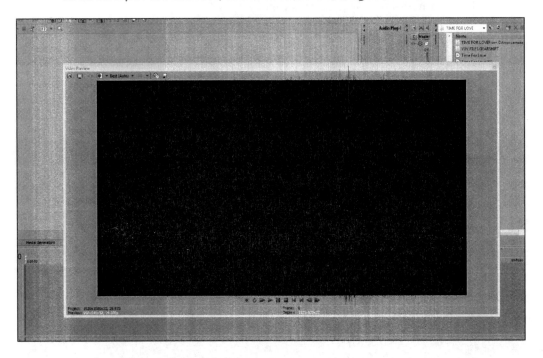

3. This free window can now be resized and positioned where ever you like on your desktop. If you had two screens attached to your computer, you could drag that window over to the second monitor.

4. So any window that has these six dots can be moved and resized independently.

5. Once you have all your windows positioned and sized to suit your working style, this unique layout can be saved into one of ten layout memory slots that are available.

6. Press *CTRL + ALT + D* and then release the keys and immediately select one of the numbers across the top of your keyboard (not your numeric pad) to save your layout into the slot. They are numbered 0 to 9, so to save in the first slot push *CTRL + ALT + D* followed by the *0* key.

7. The **Save Layout As** window will open which allows you to name your layout and decide which slot you wish to save it into:

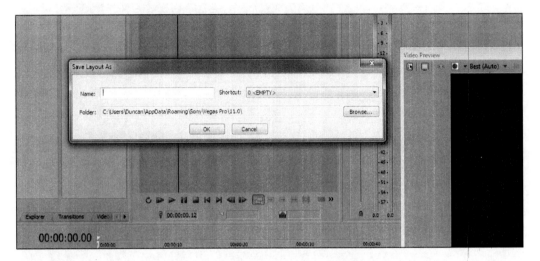

8. Give your layout a name and hit **OK** to save the layout.

9. In the future, to recall this layout you simply press *ALT + D + 0*; the last number will correspond to the save slot.

10. Sony Vegas Pro 11 comes with three preset layouts that can be found by selecting **View menu | Windows Layouts** and then choosing from **Default Layout**, **Audio Mixing**, or **Color Correction**. Or you can use the shortcuts *ALT + D + D*, *ALT + D + A*, *ALT + D + C* accordingly.

11. Even though there are only ten slots to access your layouts, an unlimited number of layouts can be saved into the Layout folder and recalled at a later date, or even imported from another computer. These can be maintained in the **Organize Layouts** menu which is found in **View | Organize Layouts**. Layouts from the current Layout folder in the left panel can be added or removed from the Layouts Menu on the right panel, as seen in the following screenshot:

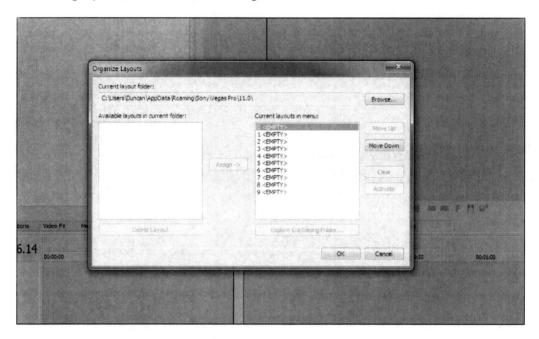

What just happened?

We now have learned the process of creating a unique Windows Layout to assist your work flow in Vegas Pro 11, as well as the ability to have 13 pre arranged layouts available to you using shortcuts, to have the windows in front of you that you need for the particular editing job you are doing.

Beginner's Guide to Vegas Pro 11 Media

As part of the *Beginner's Guide to Vegas Pro 11*, I have made available media for you to use as we work through the information and tutorials together. Once you have a full grasp of the information in each section of this book, you will be able to apply the tools to your own projects, but by using this downloaded media, you will find that the chapters will become much clearer to you far more quickly.

The project we will be working on is a Music Video clip. This kind of project is a great way to discover the powerful tools available to you in Vegas Pro 11, and apply them in a creative manner. The music bed also acts as a template that will help to guide our edits both dynamically and in the timeline.

The download files will contain a variety of video takes with scratch audio tracks and a master audio track that we will edit the video to. The files you will have downloaded are:

- Take 1
- Take 2
- Take 3
- Master Audio

The details for downloading these files are contained in the *Preface* of this book.

Video Killed the Radio Star

As the song goes "Video Killed the Radio Star," but music videos also gave birth to a whole new realm of ideas and tools along with a new league of editors specializing in an exciting creative medium. Keeping the viewer engaged and involved for about three and a half minutes doesn't sound like a hard thing to do, but in reality, keeping their attention for more than 30 seconds is a task in itself. This fact is even more relevant in today's "Instant Gratification" mind set.

So this information brings us to the first consideration we should make when planning a new Video Project. That is: "Who is our target audience?" which will then lead to the question "What format will the final video be in?".

The answer to these questions will vary from project to project, and a variety of **Video Formats** are available in Vegas Pro 11. For our Beginners' Guide Project we shall edit and render the master file in **PAL DV** format, with an **Aspect Ratio** of **16:9**, and prepare and render the final project ready to burn to a DVD playable in an everyday DVD player.

Now in the previous paragraph, I have emphasized some words and phrases that may mean nothing to the beginner, but fear not as here we will define the information to begin your Video Editing Vocabulary so you can talk it up with the best of them:

- **Video Formats**: As technology advances and more companies enter the market place to compete, they are focused on creating a new video format that is good to edit with as well as good to play back the final product. A final video file that is great for playing on YouTube wouldn't necessarily look as good as it should on a Blu-ray player. So the more companies that create new formats, the more the editing software needs to be able to handle and create. For our Music Video project, I have selected the **DV (Digital Video)** format to keep the file sizes smaller for the downloads as well as keeping the project in the same format the DVD will be created in.

> Think of it this way: A CD you buy of your favorite artist can't be just placed on top of your iPod to make it play the music. The songs on the CD have to be converted by iTunes software into an audio format that the iPod can recognize and play. Video Formats are similar to those conversions.

- **PAL**: Is an acronym that stands for **Phase Alternate Line**. This too is a form of format that defines how the vision appears on the screen. PAL is the dominant television standard in Europe and most of the world. The USA uses a different standard called NTSC, which stands for **National Television System Committee**. PAL delivers 625 lines at 50 half frames per second where as NTSC delivers 525 lines at 60 half frames per second.

- **Aspect Ratio**: This ratio represents the width and height of the picture. For many years TV was presented in the almost square ratio of 4:3, but in recent years the ratio of 16:9 has become the default standard for pretty much all projects, especially those being presented on today's big screen LCD and Plasma TVs.

Towards the end of the Vegas Pro 11 manual you will find a glossary of terms, which will also help to advance your vocabulary and understanding of the many terms used in the world of video.

Summary

In this first chapter we have set up your computer with Vegas Pro 11 and checked that we have at least the minimum system requirements.

Specifically, we covered the minimum requirements essential to run Vegas Pro 11, where to find the built-in help and tutorials as well as the location of online help. We then explored the windows of the Vegas 11 Interface, and we also started to enrich your Video Vocabulary by addressing some common terms

We have lightly touched on most of the windows in Vegas Pro 11, so that you may start to know your way around this impressive software. I have always believed the best way to learn a software package is to actually use it in a project. So with that thought we can move forward and start to get our teeth into the ins and outs and personality traits of our new friend Vegas Pro 11.

2
Let the Magic Begin: Beginning the Project and Acquiring Media

As we progress through this guide, I will add new methods and knowledge to your arsenal of tools. Each new chapter will call on the knowledge of the previous one to help advance you as an experienced Vegas Pro editor. As with any new software, using it in an actual project will always help you to remember the tools you have used, so now that we have a better grasp of the user interface of Vegas Pro 11, it is time to jump right in and start the project at hand.

In this chapter, we shall discuss:

- ◆ Creating a project
- ◆ Project Properties
- ◆ Standard Definition versus High Definition
- ◆ Pixel Aspect Ratio
- ◆ The Preview Monitor
- ◆ Importing media clips
- ◆ Importing from other sources
- ◆ The Smart tool and media clips
- ◆ Keyboard Shortcuts

So let's get on with it...

Creating a project

Before we start any project we have to establish its properties. These property values are essential to ensure that the finished product will be played back correctly on the delivery-method format. For example, if you are based in the USA, you will probably need your project to conform to the NTSC format, whereas Europe and the rest of the world would use the PAL format. Playing NTSC-formatted files on a PAL system will either cause the file not to play, or have strange anomalies occur, such as stretching the pictures height.

Project Properties

The **Project Properties** window seen in the following screenshot can be accessed by selecting the **File** menu and choosing **Properties** or by pressing *ALT + ENTER*:

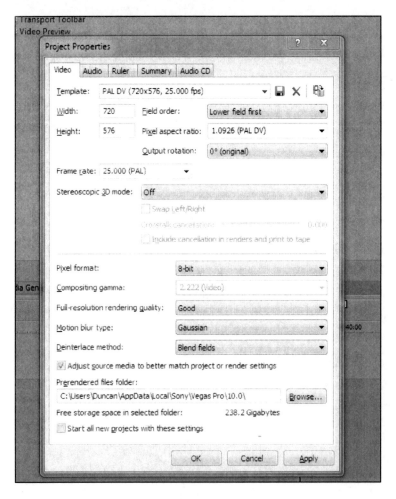

Go ahead and open the **Project Properties** window. Across the top of the **Project Properties** window you will see five tabs. Under the **Video** tab the first information box is called **Template**. Inside this drop-down box you will find a comprehensive list of templates. Usually, one of these templates will do the job perfectly for you, but knowing what the templates contain is needed before you can decide. Let's cover the important information and fields you need to know.

Standard Definition versus High Definition

The fast paced times we live in has seen the video production world going through some major changes due to advances in technology. Especially in the new worlds of Home Theatre, High Definition TVs, DVD and Blu-ray players, Web-based Television and podcasts, as well as Digital Cinema. Thankfully, Sony Vegas Pro 11 has all of these possible formats covered within its Project Properties Templates.

Way back in the early days of editing, we only had Standard Definition TV and Academy of Cinema Film editing formats to worry about, but now there are many formats, resolutions, and screen sizes to consider. The following chart will give you an idea of most of the screen resolutions being used, and their relationships in size with each other:

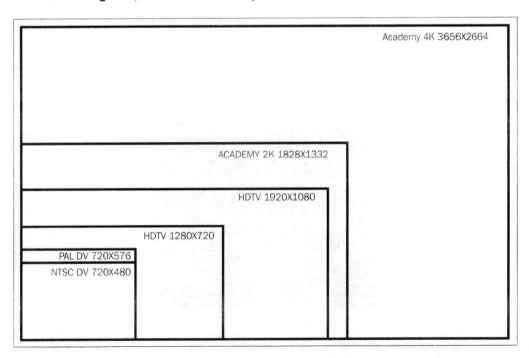

As you can see, the physical screen sizes vary greatly, which also increases the amount of data being stored both on hard drives and recordable media, such as DVD or Blu-ray.

Depending where you live in the world, DVD video is expressed as DV (either PAL or NTSC) and can be in WIDESCREEN format for a 16:9, **Pixel Aspect Ratio**. This has become the default resolution for DVD creation, especially due to the size limitation of the data that can be held by the DVD. A standard DVD can only hold about 4.7 gigabytes of data and a dual Layer DVD can hold close to 8.5 gigabytes. Even at these media data sizes, the video needs to be compressed using a **Codec** (a mathematical algorithm to make the files smaller, deriving its name from the two words compressor and decompressor) to allow a complete movie to fit onto a single disk. Today, the increase in the amount of data needed for HD Video helped to give birth to the BLU-RAY DISK format, where a single layer disk can hold around 25 gigabytes, and a dual layer around 50 gigabytes. A compression codec is still used, but these newer codec types leave very little effect or artefacts behind in the video on the final disk.

Pixel Aspect Ratio

There are a couple of ways that the **Pixel Aspect Ratio (PAR)** setting is represented. Generally, the term aspect ratio refers to the ratio of a picture's width to its height. If the aspect ratio of a picture is 1:1, the width and height would be the same, and you'd have a square. Standard PAL video has an aspect ratio of 4:3. That means for every four units width you have three units height, where as 16:9 will have 16 units width to 9 units in height. This ratio is also often defined as a decimal point number. For example, PAL DV WIDESCREEN has a PAR of 1.4568 where as the PAL DV template has a PAR of 1.0926, but you will note that both templates have the same Width and Height of 720 and 576. A TV and/or computer screen is represented by a certain number of pixels, and in both cases the DV picture is 720 pixels wide and 576 pixels high, but ends up being a different screen shape. See the following screenshot:

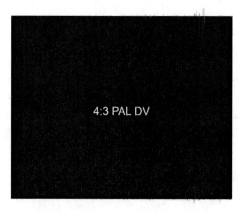

4:3 PAL DV

The difference lies in the shape of the individual pixels. Like the overall screen, the pixels are square for 4:3 as in the previous screenshot, and rectangular for 16:9 as in the next screenshot:

That is, the pixels are the same shape as the screens. For HD footage, the Pixel Aspect Ratio is simply defined as 1.3333 (HDV 1080). All HD footage regardless of field order, width and height, or frame rate, will be defined as 16:9 or 1.3333. Thankfully, as the Television technology is developing, most new HD TVs can deliver all of the possible formats correctly.

FIELD ORDER

This property is derived from the difference of pictures on film and pictures on TV. In reference to PAL, a piece of film is equivalent to 25 frames (pictures) per second, whereas TV was designed to be broadcast over the airwaves as 50 separate half pictures that were stitched together at the receiver to create the 25 complete frames. This stitching together of the 25 pairs of the 50 pictures was referred to as **Interlacing** the picture. This was the birth of the terms **Progressive** footage (**Film**) and **Interlaced** footage (**TV**). You may have heard of the terms regarding new HD TVs as being able to produce 1080i or 1080p where the "i" and "p" refer to Interlaced and Progressive respectively. Some editors have a preference out of the two formats saying that Progressive gives a more "filmic" experience, whereas others prefer the interlaced format. Even though film may have never been used in the production of a broadcast video, if delivered in Progressive format, it is a sequence of 25 complete pictures that is used to achieve the result.

FRAME RATE

Hailing back to the days of film, frame rate specifies how many frames per second are shown. As the options in **Project Properties** show, PAL is 25, NTSC is 29.97 and if the end product is to be transferred back to film for it to be projected, then 24 FPS is necessary.

MATCH MEDIA SETTINGS

On the far right of the **Video** tab in line with the template options you will find a small icon, circled in red in the following screenshot:

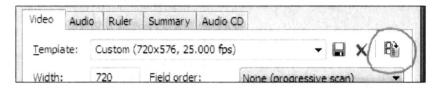

This small button can be a great way to set up the preferences in one quick process. If you have shot or received your footage in the same format that you intend to finish the project, then you can use one of the clips to define Project Properties. I have supplied the footage for our Beginners' Guide Project in the format we need to finalize it in. So let's use this function to set up our Project Properties.

Time for action – using the supplied clips to set Project Properties

We are going to use one of the video clips that you have downloaded for the beginner's guide project, to set up the Project Properties:

1. Start Vegas Pro 11, and once open, from the menu select **File | New** to create a new project.

2. Once created, use **File | Save As**, name the project **Video Tutorial**, and save it in the same location that you have placed the downloaded Tutorial Project media files.

3. From the menu again select **File | Properties** and the **Project Properties** box will open.

4. Select the **Match Media Settings** button we spoke about earlier and use the **Look In** explorer to find and select **Take 1** of the downloaded files. Once highlighted, choose **Open**.

5. To finish use **File | Save** to save your settings.

6. If you look at the **Project Properties** window, the properties should now have changed to look like the following:

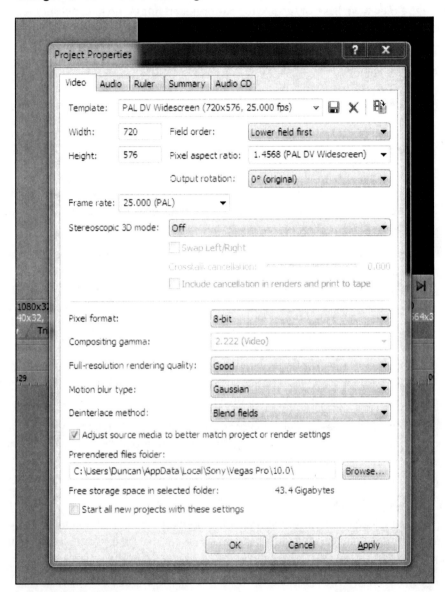

What just happened?

By using the properties of the supplied video clips, and using the Match Media Settings function, we have set up Project Properties for our Project in a format that will be best suited to burning our final, edited project to a standard DVD.

Time for action – setting Project Properties from scratch

Sometime the media we have or receive for our project is not in the final delivery format, therefore we need to be able to select the correct settings.

We shall now set Project Properties from scratch, using our knowledge of the intended video format to set the values:

1. Start Vegas Pro 11, and once open, from the menu select **File | New** to create a new project.

2. Once created, use **File | Save As** and name the project what you would like. Save it in the directory of your choice.

3. By taking into consideration what our final video format will be, we can start to set the needed Project Properties. From the menu again select **File | Properties** and the **Project Properties** window will open.

4. We have decided that our final project will be burnt to Blu-ray, and is a Full High Definition format. Select the down arrow at the end of the Template window and look through the options available. Select **HD 1080-50i (1920x1080, 25.000 fps)**. Keep in mind that starting your project in the highest resolution required is a good thing, as it is then easier to downgrade the parameters to a lower resolution for say DVD, Internet playback, or Podcast, depending on the client's later decisions.

5. You will notice that all of the parameters are now set to the correct values. This means that no matter what format any media you bring into the session is, it will show you how this will look at the final resolution.

6. The Template values available in Vegas Pro 11 cover pretty much any option you may need, but even then, you can go through all of the parameters and set them to whatever value you wish to suit your creative output.

What just happened?

By using our knowledge and understanding of required formats in addition to knowing what our final video will be viewed in, we applied one of the available templates to set the Project Properties.

Tip: For those wishing to delve even more deeply into the Project Properties, use the Interactive and Online tutorials that are under the **Help Menu** in Sony Vegas Pro 11.

Pop quiz – formats

Which of the following Project Properties would be incorrect if my video was to be burned to a PAL DVD disk?

a.   Width of 720 pixels

b.   Height of 576 pixels

c.   Pixel aspect ratio of 1.4568

d.   Frame rate of 24.000 frames per second

The Preview Monitor

Before we import our media into our newly-created project, I want to bring your attention to the Preview monitor. This preview screen is where you will be seeing the output of your editing and the effects you apply to your media clips. Ideally, you will have a second screen attached to your editing computer where you can either move the Preview monitor onto or where you can use the **Video Preview on External Monitor** function. If you are using one screen, then you will need to resize the Preview Monitor where you are able to clearly see your edits, but at the same time, leave enough acreage on your screen to be able to work with your media on the timeline.

In the previous image, you can see at the top of the Preview monitor a series of buttons. The **x**, **<**, and row of dots at the top-left are for closing the Preview monitor, sliding the monitor out of the way of other windows, and for grabbing and holding the monitor window to detach and move it around your desktop, respectively.

The next square with the mouse icon in it is another way to open the Project Properties window. The little Blue Monitor is to send the preview video to an external monitor. If you select from the menu **Options | Preferences** and select the **Preview Device** tab, you can choose which device you wish to use as your external monitor. For a second computer screen, you would select **Windows Secondary Display** from the device drop-down window. Once this is set up, by clicking the little Blue Monitor your preview will also appear on the second screen for a larger preview as well as the Monitor Preview window.

To the right of the Blue Monitor button is the Sony standard symbol for FX plugins. Here you can insert Video FX over the Preview Monitor such as a color correction plugin to help calibrate the colors of your monitor.

The **Split Screen** view button is a great way to compare what an effect is doing to your video. One half will be affected while the other half remains unaffected for your comparison.

The **Preview Quality** drop-down is an important menu to get to know. Within this there are four main settings: **Draft, Preview, Good,** and **Best** with subheadings under each including **Auto, Full, Half,** and **Quarter**. Depending on the CPU and video card power available on your system, certain combinations of these settings work the best. The system defaults to Preview (Auto), which should give very adequate monitoring, but as you add FX plugins to your project and more edits and cuts to the timeline, the system starts to become taxed and will need to drop the Monitor preview quality. We will leave it as the default setting for now.

The **Overlays** button is essential when creating video for TV, particularly the Safe Areas grid setting. By keeping your main content between the safe area lines and the center of the screen, the zoom in effect (or over scan) of some TVs won't cut off some of your important text or on-screen action.

Finally, the last two buttons allow you to grab still images from the preview screen. The first saves the image to the clipboard allowing you to paste it into your photo editing software, and the second saves the image to your location of choice on your hard drive for recall later. You can select between JPG and PNG formats to save your images. Obviously set your Preview Quality to **Best Full** for the highest quality image before taking the snapshot.

Importing media clips

Importing media clips into the project is a fairly easy function to use. Here we will bring the video and audio clips needed for our Project into the timeline. As we have already established the Project Properties previously, all we need to do now is to select the explorer window just above the Track Header and use the usual windows explorer functions to find our downloaded files. You should find **Take 1**, **Take 2**, **Take 3**, and **Master Audio**.

Time for action – importing media

After ensuring that we have our **Video Tutorial** project open, we can start the media import process:

1. Click and hold Take 1 and drag it down to the timeline. You will see the outline box of the clip appear showing you the leading edge of the clip. Drag the clip so it is hard against the left of the timeline and let it go.

2. Click your mouse in the grey area below the Take 1 clip and then while holding the *Alt* key, scroll your mouse wheel (if you have one) to zoom out so you can see the complete length of the clip. If you don't have a mouse wheel, never fear as there are always at least a few ways to do pretty much every function in Vegas Pro 11. In the bottom right corner of the timeline window you will see a + and – button on the horizontal bar. Continue to click the – button to zoom out and see the whole clip.

3. If the clip isn't hard against the left-hand wall of the timeline, left click and hold and drag the clip to the left till it can't move anymore and let it go. You will notice that once the clip is in place, the track header to the left of the clip now contains controller buttons and a level slider which all pertain to that clip.

4. There is a gray box on the track header just above the Level 100 % text. Double click in this gray box and type the name **Take 1** and hit enter. You have now named the track.

5. Now repeat the process with the remaining two video files and place them underneath the first track, remembering to name the tracks as well.

6. Once that is complete you can now do the same process to the master audio clip. Everything will be exactly the same as the video clips except that it will create an audio track instead of a video track with its own set of buttons, volume control, and pan control sliders. It will also contain a VU meter to show you the level of the audio on playback.

7. Once you have all of the media in place, rewind the project by using the Rewind to start button at the bottom of the screen on the transport controls or press the *CTRL + HOME* keys. Your preview window will now be black as the first frame of the clips, are black. Ensuring your speakers aren't turned up too loud, press the **space bar** and watch and listen to the project.

8. What you are seeing is the top track, **Take 1** playing. Even though Take 2 and 3 are also playing they cannot be seen, as the highest video track takes preference. While the track is still playing, on the track header of Take 1 click on the white circle with a gray line through it. That is the mute button. It will mute the first track and what you now see on the Preview screen is Take 2.

9. Alternatively, select the exclamation symbol on Take 2. This is the **Solo** button which will mute the other two video tracks and only show the track you have selected Solo for. Note that the video Solo buttons don't interfere with the audio track playback.

10. Lastly, select from the menu bar **File | Save** or press **CTRL + S** to save your project. Always a good habit to get into is to press **CTRL + S** after you do something or make a change. After a while it will become second nature. If for some reason your system loses power or locks up, Vegas Pro 11 has an automatic function that saves the session. Then the next time you open Vegas Pro 11, it will ask if you want to restore this last automatically saved version. I still like to make my own saved copies as I work. I guess it is just a good habit I have acquired working with computers over the years. Occasionally the auto saved version isn't as up-to-date as my personally-saved version, so I have found it very helpful. As with any project you work with over an extended period of time, it is advisable to make a backup copies of the Vegas Pro 11 session and all of its associated media files on a backup drive in case of hard drive failure. There is nothing worse than losing two months of hard work and edits because a hard drive fails.

11. Your Vegas Project should look something like the following screenshot:

What just happened?

You have just successfully imported the required media files for our project. As you watch and listen to the video tracks by using the Solo buttons on each track, ensure that the vocals audio and the lip movement of the singer are in sync. If not, ensure that all four of the clips are as far to the left of the timeline against the left wall as possible. This will ensure the lipsync of the music video is correct.

Moving on...

Importing from other sources

Although this tutorial has the media supplied in a digital format that makes importing an easy process, from time to time you will need to bring your media into your project from a variety of sources. This will be dependent upon things such as what kind of camera you are using, or even media formats the media is supplied to you in, such as XDCAM. Here we will discuss some of these options.

Import

If you have a client that supplies you with media that needs to be edited on an external hard drive, you may wish to import that media into the session. Although it is okay to drag and drop media clips onto the timeline, this isn't necessarily a good idea with a lot of clips, especially if they are in a different kind of format or even a variety of formats. Under the **File** menu you will find an **Import** menu that gives you four choices: **Media**, **Broadcast Wave Format**, **DVD Camcorder Disc**, and **Closed Captioning**. Although the last three are of a particular media type, the **Import Media** menu will open up the **Import Media** window, which allows you to point the system to an external hard drive, or other device depending on where the files are stored:

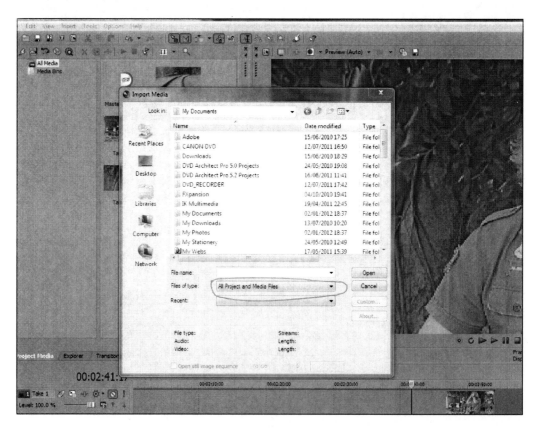

Inside the **Files of type** drop-down menu circled in the previous image, you will find pretty much every media type available from **Vegas Project Files** to **XDCAM EX MP4** files, and everything in between. Here you can select multiple files and import them into our Project Media bin. If the client can't leave the hard drive or device with you, then first copy all of the files onto your editing hard drive before importing them into the project. If you import them from the client's drive and they take it away after the session, the next time you open the session the project won't be able to find the files and will leave them offline and unviewable.

Another special file format is the **XDCAM** format. Usually if you are dealing with XDCAM files you will be looking at them directly on the **SONY XDCAM** camera's hard drive or removable drive disk. Vegas Pro 11 has a XDCAM Explorer window specifically for importing these files. With the XDCAM device connected to your system you can open **XDCAM Explorer**. Here, the files can be selected and imported into both your session and onto your system's editing hard drive:

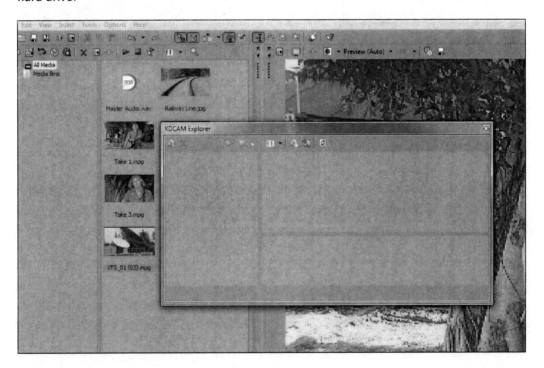

If you have a camera that records to digital tape in DV or HDV format or are presented with one, then the footage needs to be imported into the system and into the project. Once again *Sony Vegas Pro 11* provides a dedicated Capture Video window. Under the **File** menu select **Capture Video.** You will be presented with the option window to select if your tape format is **DV** or **HDV/SDI**.

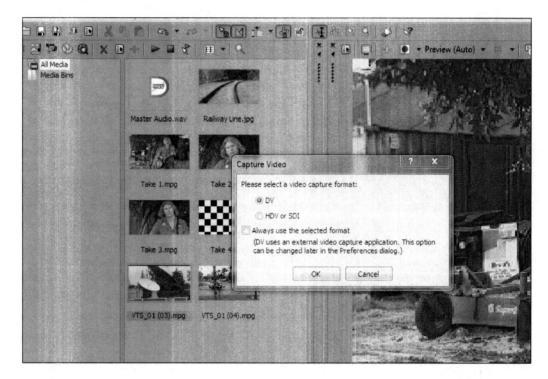

Select the format appropriate to your camera and the appropriate Sony Video Capture application will open. This will allow you to take control of your camera to select and import the footage to your system and project. As this is a real-time process, you can watch the importing footage on the in-built monitoring window. The following screenshot shows the HDV/SDI Capture window:

This window allows you to select the footage you wish to capture as the video plays, as well as defining where you wish the files to be stored on your system and to allocate a name for that particular set of captured files.

As you can see, Sony Vegas Pro 11 has allowed for pretty much every file type available to you for importing into your project. One of the beauties of this editing software is that it allows you to have different formats on the timeline that can all be edited and rendered out to a final format easily.

What just happened?

We have just touched on some of the main methods for importing media and footage into your project. As you do more editing and projects, you may be presented with a variety of different formats to contend with, but you will have the confidence to know that Vegas Pro 11 can deal with pretty much anything that is thrown at you. The Sony Vegas help centre is a great place to go (it can be found under the **Help** menu) to cover these and other methods in more detail.

The Smart tool and media clips

Now that we have the media clips on the timeline, let's have a look at the ways we can manipulate these events:

- ◆ **Cropping tool**

   The mouse cursor in Vegas Pro 11 acts as a smart tool when on the timeline. If you hover the mouse near the centre of **Take 1** at the leading edge, you will see the cursor change to a square with a double-headed arrow pointing left and right. This is the **Cropping tool**.

   This tool allows you to slide the leading edge (or tail edge if you choose that end) of the clip along the media clip. In effect you are shortening or lengthening the clip to start or end at a new location within the clip.

   You will also note that the preview window updates your selected video to show you the actual location you are selecting or moving to. Go ahead and try this tool remembering to stop playback and return the clip back to its original fully extended position when you are finished. You could also use the Windows standard *CTRL + Z* undo function repeatedly until it moves back to its original state.

   If you go to the end of the clip and slide the cropping tool past this point, you will see that the clip creates an indent at the top edge to show you where the end is, but the clip extends itself and starts to play from the beginning again, creating a loop. This can be useful for bringing a small media clip or still image into the timeline and then looping it for as long as you like.

◆ **Fade Offset tool**

If you now hover your mouse over the top-left or top-right corner of your media clip, you will see a quadrant appear with a double-headed arrow pointing left and right. This is the **Fade Offset tool**. By clicking and sliding this tool you will create a fade in (or fade out if you chose the end of clip). Create a fade in (top-left corner of Take 1). Once done press the *CTRL + HOME* keys to take the cursor back to beginning and then press the *space bar* to play the clip. You will see **Take 1** fade in over **Take 2**. This fade can be as long or as short as you like. If you right-click the mouse in the middle of the fade, a list of options will appear. Select the first option **Fade Type** and you will see that you can choose from a variety of fade curve types that may suit your creative choices. Once done, stop playback and bring the clip back to its original state without a fade. Do this by clicking the highest point of the Fade Curve and sliding it back to the edge of the clip again. You could also use the Windows standard *CTRL + Z* undo function repeatedly until it moves back to its original state:

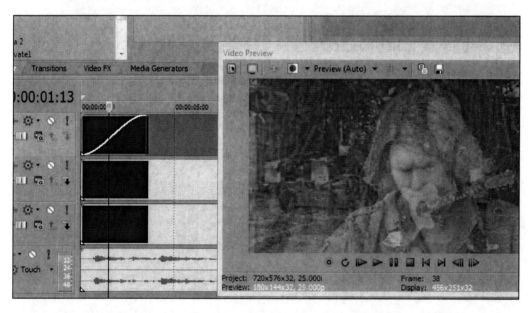

◆ **Opacity tool**

Moving your mouse to the top edge of **Take 1**, you will see a pointed hand appear. This tool will allow you to pull down the **Opacity** (or transparency) of the take. If you pull the opacity down to around 50 % you will notice that you can see both **Take 1** and **Take 2** playing together if you push play again. This can be a useful tool for creating overlay effects or any creative idea you can think of. Once again return the clip to its original state once you have finished trying out the tool.

◆ **Splitting or cutting media clips**

First, let's position our mouse about halfway along the **Take 1** clip in the middle of the clip and left-click. This will move the timeline cursor to this location. Now if we press the *S* key on our keyboard, you will see that **Take 1** media clip has been cut into two separate pieces, each with their own FX and Event Crop icon on them. You can click and hold the right-hand clip and slide it on the timeline to see that it is now a separate clip. As you bring it back into place, you will notice the join of the two clips turns into a *blue highlight* to let you know they are now touching each other. If you continue to slide the clip to the left, the two clips will overlap each other and create a crossfade, with a *purple highlight* appearing once the cross fade is exactly 1 second long:

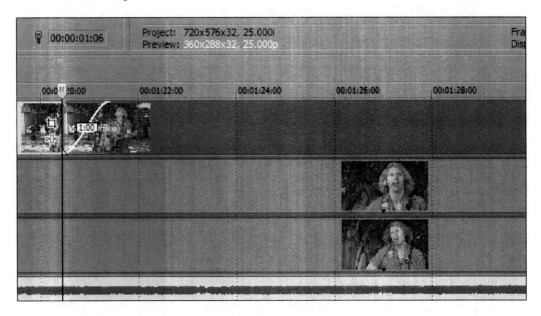

Just like in Fade Types, if you right-click in the middle of the crossfade you just created, options will appear and if you select the **Fade Type** menu a whole new list of cross fade types will appear for your selection. Let's return the clip to its original position but keep the split active. Slide the right-hand clip to the right until the blue line appears at the join. Once the blue line appears, then you know the two clips are touching at the split point.

◆ **Event Pan/Crop tool**

You may have noticed at the right-hand end of the Video media clip there are two icons sitting on the clips. The bottom one is the standard Sony FX icon for **Event FX**, which we will deal with in the effects section of this book, and the top one is the **Event Pan/Crop** tool. Let's click on the Event Pan/Crop tool icon on the right-hand clip of the split clip of **Take 1.** The **Event Pan/Crop** window will open showing us the very first frame of the media clip we have selected. This window will have a list of parameters on the left, and the scene will have a bounding box around it with the letter **F** overlaid in the middle of it. You will also find a small timeline and cursor along the bottom. For those wondering about the overlay **F**, it allows us to know if an abstract picture is inverted or not:

Position and resize the **Event Pan/Crop** and **Preview Monitor** windows so you can see them both, which will allow you to see the changes you are making with this tool. If you are using the External Monitor Preview function, this won't be an issue for you.

In the **Event Pan/Crop** window, you will notice there are eight little squares on the bounding box around the frame. With your mouse, grab the top-left corner box and drag it towards the centre of the picture. Watch the Preview monitor as you do this and you will see that it acts like a zoom. If you then move the box out past the frame, it zooms out making the picture smaller than the frame. This can be a useful tool to remove unwanted objects that were included during filming or to make the take look like it was shot from another camera pass closer to the subject:

As this zooming in is actually spreading less pixels over the same area of the frame, there is a limit to the amount of resizing you can do before the picture begins to look grainy or pixeled. If we were using HD footage with a resolution of 1920 x 1080, then there would be a lot more pixels covering the frame, so it would allow for greater resizing before the artefacts became apparent. Now let's zoom the picture in a fair way. Once the zoom is where you like it, click the mouse on the main timeline on **Take 1** just to the left of the split point. Press the *space bar* and watch the preview window as the cursor travels forward through the split point. You will see that the preview jumps to the newly-zoomed scene and will stay there right through to the end of the clip. You can create multiple splits on a clip and resize or zoom each of the clips you create to their own individual setting.

To bring the frame back to normal size, from the **Preset** drop-down window at the top of the **Event Crop/Pan** window, select **Default**.

Now, if you move the mouse just above or beside the Bounding Box a circular rotation icon will appear. This tool allows us to rotate the frame just like we had filmed the scene with the camera rotated to one side or the other:

Once again give this tool a try by clicking and holding the mouse and moving it up or down. Your changes will appear in the preview window. Return the image back to its default setting by selecting it in the Preset drop-down once you have finished looking at this tool.

As you make these changes, you will notice that all the parameters to the left of the frame will change to represent your moves numerically. You can also enter numbers into the parameters to make the changes. When you click on a parameter a drop-down slider will appear to allow you to modify the settings in this manner. If you notice the parameters under the **Position** heading, you will see that the **Width** and **Height** are represented as **720** and **576**, accordingly. So this tells us that the unit of this parameter is pixels as the clip we are using is a PAL DV Clip which has the exact same width and height:

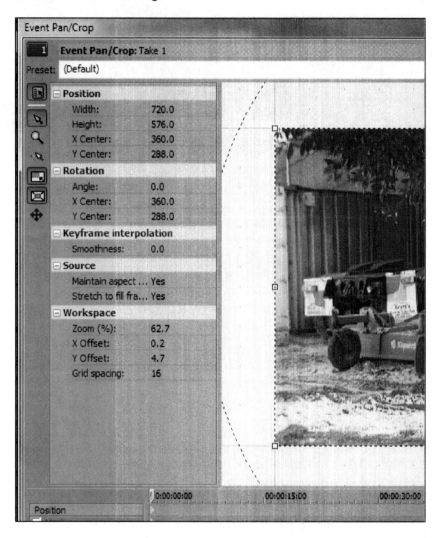

Also a handy function is to save the settings you have made as a preset. Once you have the scene looking as you like it, you can save it for use with other clips by clicking on the little Floppy Disk icon on the right-hand side of the Preset drop-down window after naming your preset. The next time you look into the drop-down preset list you will see your newly-saved preset available to apply to any clip using the **Event Pan/Crop** window.

I would advise you to name your presets with a name that will help you to remember what the preset represents. By doing this, over time you will have a great list of presets that you can utilize on your future projects to help speed up your editing process.

Tip: Commit this Preset Saving process to memory as it is utilized in many of the windows we will be encountering as we travel through the tools available to use in Vegas Pro 11.

Keyboard Shortcuts

As is the case with most modern computer tools, there is a myriad of ways of doing the same job efficiently. Some editors prefer to use the mouse while others find keyboard shortcuts an invaluable asset. Personally I like to use a combination of the two.

To help you discover these shortcuts go to the **Help** menu in Vegas Pro 11 and select **Keyboard Shortcuts** for a concise list of these valuable shortcuts.

Tip: It might even pay you to print this list out and keep it next to your editing station until you can commit the essential ones to memory.

Summary

We have covered a lot of information here regarding your media clips on the timeline. From the Preview monitor that helps you to see your edits in addition to importing clips to the timeline, which is essential to begin our project. We also discussed Smart tools you can use to manipulate and change your clips in a physical way, as well as how to create fades and crossfades on your media clips and splitting and sliding clips on the timeline

We looked at the **Event Pan/Crop** tool for resizing, zooming in and out, clip rotation, and the Saving Presets process in the **Event Pan/Crop** window, which works for all presets in all windows.

Getting to know all of these tools intimately will certainly give you an editing advantage and increase your speed during the editing process. These tools are the building blocks on which we will begin to expand and build your skill set for editing.

So let's continue on our journey of building your relationship with Vegas Pro 11 and dig deeper into the toolset that awaits you within this powerful software.

Onward and forward to Chapter 3.

3

Video Editing Concepts and Application

Editing video is a critically important part of the video creation process. It's the place where all of the preliminary concepts you had for your video at the beginning of the project, come together. The process is so important that the Academy Of Motion Pictures gives out an Academy Award for Best Editor every year. Here we will learn some of the history of this specialized skill set and apply some of these concepts to our project. This process will also take us deeper into the settings and parameters of the tools we have been looking at.

The topics we shall cover include:

◆ A light history of editing that is cutting film, splicing film, and the language of editing

◆ Video editing: What makes a good edit / cut and how to do it

◆ Multicamera tool

◆ Event panning and cropping tool

◆ Slow and fast motion

So let's get on with it...

Beginner's Guide Tutorial Project

To effectively get the most from this chapter, you will need to have the project we started in the previous chapter accessible, as we will continue to edit our Music Video clip. Once we start the *Time for Action* section, you will need to open the project to work on.

Editing: A light history lesson

In the early days of film, editing was something that was done pretty much while the footage was being shot, in the camera. So, often the cuts between one scene and the next were simply the spot where the camera was stopped and then started again. Also the attitude towards creating a movie was to make it lifelike and realtime, which consequentially lead to very long scenes with cuts and edits that felt un-natural and in effect were a very obvious jolt to the senses of the viewer. As the audience back then was new to the experience of watching a film, they were happy to sit through these long, jerky feeling movies, just to have the experience of being entertained.

Today, audiences are very savvy and extremely experienced at being a viewer. Whether they realize it or not, they have been educated over their whole life as to certain editing tricks and formulas that have become a language or dialogue between the film maker/editor and their audience. For example, a dream sequence or a dialogue in a movie that is set in the past is often presented in black and white or sepia (old fashioned tan/bronze color), which the audience automatically associates with the past. The sun and clouds presented in time-lapse footage often refers to the passage of time, just as in some older films the clock or calendar flashing quickly through hours and days does.

As film producers realized they could physically cut the film and re-stick it back together (splice) in a different order to which it was filmed, a whole new world of movie making began. Storylines no longer had to be confined to a fixed timeline, and this allowed screenplay writers to be far more creative with their storytelling. This is also the time when the position of editors became a recognized and rewarded part of the process. The editors themselves became the translator of the story in the directors head into a language that the viewer would understand and enjoy.

So a language has been created that you the editor need to learn to make the story being told by the video a smooth and comfortable experience for the viewer. The trick of course is to use these editing tools in a way that creates familiarity, but also with a touch of creativity. If you re-watch one of your favorite movies, but this time watch it with an analytical eye to see where some of these editing tools have been used to convey the story better, you will start to become aware of the language you didn't realize you already knew.

Using the *Tutorial Project* we saved in the last chapter, let's make some edits and cuts to our media on the timeline and see how it affects the feel and the flow of our music video.

Time for action – creating a second version of our project

We will be exploring two different methods of creating edits and cuts to our project in this chapter, so before we start the process we need to save two versions:

1. Open Vegas Pro 11.

2. Select **File Menu | Open** and find our video Tutorial Project and open it. The Project we saved called **Video Tutorial** may still be in the recently opened files at the bottom of the **File Menu** list. If so select it.

3. Once the project is opened, choose from the menu, **File | Save as**, and rename the file as **Multicamera** and save again.

4. Once saved, return to **File | Open** and select our first project again and open **Video Tutorial** ready to start our edits.

What just happened?

Since we will be exploring two different methods of editing and cutting our media, we need to have two versions of our project saved at the same point in time. By saving the project under a new name called Multicamera, we can load this project at a later time and begin editing from the same starting point as our Video Tutorial project.

What makes a good edit or cut

Editing or cutting and splicing film was a physical process where an actual blade was used to cut the film into segments. That allowed these segments to be shortened and or moved to a different location in the timeline of the movie and spliced back together. This process was performed on machines as shown in the following screenshots:

Thankfully today, editing video is a lot easier and lacks the stress and worry of getting it wrong by cutting the film in the wrong place or, destroying an irreplaceable scene that can't be shot again. The advent of computers means that all of our edits are undoable, as well as being non linear, which simply means that we don't have to roll the film all the way to the end to cut out a piece of footage and then wind it back onto the spool again to place it near the beginning. Our modern timeline means we can select moments anywhere on the timeline and edit to our heart's content. Some would argue that this also means we can over think and over edit when we should have had a storyboard and a screenplay in place to work to before we even started the filming process. In reality, budget and lack of time leads us to grab the camera, shoot what we can, and fix it in the edit. Having said that, I know nothing beats good planning and writing in the creative process.

Editing isn't always just to change timelines, but also to create a flow or a visual way to guide the viewer through the story of the video from start to finish. If you think about it, in real life we see everything through our eyes in real time, and not in the un-natural way that video is presented. For example, if we were to watch a couple meeting for the first time, we have to see and listen to all the preliminary nervous conversation and the finding of their comfort zones, all the idle chatter topics, letting down of their guards, and so on. This process could take three hours to unfold in reality, whereas in a movie this whole procedure may only take up to two minutes or less. By using different camera angles, and **Point-of-View (POV)** shots of their faces, we can represent their relationship quickly unfolding. In the first scene they may be seated a distance apart but in the next shot, they may be seated very closely together. The viewer immediately knows that they are becoming more comfortable, and with the growing pile of empty glasses on the table in front of them suggesting that they have already had a few drinks together, which also infers the passing of time. Suddenly in the last scene you may find them both lying in bed smoking a cigarette together, which has been for a long time a visual euphemism for the fact that an intimate interchange has taken place. This whole relationship process, which may in reality have taken a whole night or even a few weeks to take place, can now be presented in a few minutes through the magic of multiple camera shots, scenes, and edits.

Our project at hand is a little different to the one mentioned above in that it is a music video clip. But in a similar manner we need to make the three minutes or so of the song passing by do so in a way that the viewer will find interesting as well as keeping them engaged. This music video is mostly about the performance of the song, but there is an element of storytelling involved. In this case the story is not the one of the song's lyrics alone, but includes in part the story of the making of the song and the performer's enjoyment and involvement in that process. At the same time, the viewer also wants to see the singer's passion and delivery of the song as the stories unfold.

As we edit, references will be made to the timeline and positions on it. These time references are of the format 00:01:58:12 where each pair of numbers starting from the left refer to hours, minutes, seconds, and frames. So a timeline number stating 00:01:58:12 means a position on the timeline that is 1 minute 58 seconds and 12 frames from the beginning of the timeline. Depending on your base format time reference, the frames are expressed in increments of 24 frames per second, which is a film standard. In my part of the world (Australia), I generally use the PAL standard of 25 frames per second for Broadcast Productions unless my project will end up on film.

Time for action – selecting edit points in our media clips

With our Tutorial project session open, we can start to select edits that will work to make our music video clip present well. The first step in this process is to mark any actual problems in each take that may need to be removed. Problems such as footage with digital glitches, annoying factors like hair blowing in a distracting way, and objects that are in the frame that shouldn't be there such as crew, microphones, lights, and so on. To be a great editor, you need to make yourself very familiar with the footage you have at hand to edit. Some accomplish this by watching each take through several times from start to finish and noting any good or bad things that exist in the "Take" or "Media Clip" that needs to be either removed or kept, along with making note of the timeline reading that the event happens at. For example, if we solo the Take 1 track, and move our timeline to 1 minute 48 seconds (that is 00:01:48:00), you will notice that the singer brushes his hair off his face then one of the crew steps in from the left and adjusts the hair of the singer in the clip. Obviously this section needs to be removed. Let's do exactly that:

1. Click the Solo button on the track header of Take 1. This will ensure you are looking at that track only.

2. In the middle of the Take 1 media clip, click the position that reads 00:01:48:00 on the timeline.

3. Press the *S* key on your keyboard to make a split at this point as shown in the next screenshot:

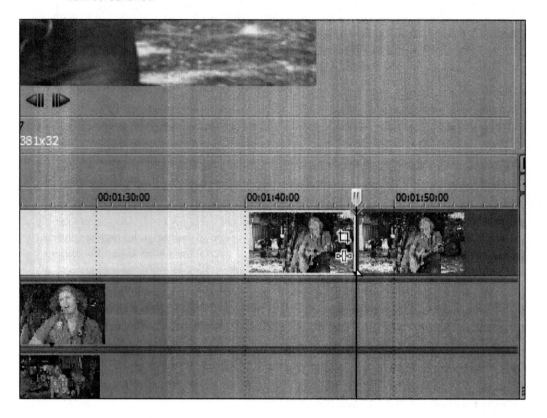

4. Once you have made the split point, press the *space bar* to play the clip from that point and see how much of the clip you need to remove. You will see that the next split point will be needed at 00:02:01:00 just after the crew member exits the screen.

5. Ensuring the cursor is at 00:02:01:00 press the *S* key again to make a second split point.

6. Now press the left mouse button on the Take 1 media anywhere between the two split points we just created and that section of the clip will be highlighted.

7. We can now remove this unwanted piece of media by deleting it via the *Delete* key on your keyboard or by using *Ctrl + X* keys

8. Our preview monitor will now go black and we will see a gap in the Take 1 media as shown in the next screenshot:

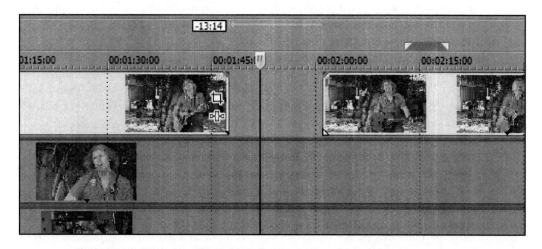

9. Now uncheck or turn off the Solo button on the Take 1 header and place the cursor just before our newly-created gap. Press the *space bar* to play the video and you will see in the preview monitor that the playback jumps from Take 1 to Take 2 and back again, successfully removing the unwanted footage and keeping the flow of the video happening. It is not unusual for us to see the camera change from a long shot such as Take 1 to a medium shot as in Take 2 and back again.

10. Now that we have started to cut our takes into multiple clips, we need to be sure that we don't slide our whole media clips forward or backward on the timeline as this will put our video out-of-sync with the audio, which will make the singer's lip sync incorrect. Definitely not a good look for a music video clip!

 In this next section, if you are having trouble getting the end of the clip to change to the correct timeline number, you may need to deselect **Enable Snapping** from the **Options Menu** or alternatively use the *F8* key. This will allow you to move the ends of the clips frame-by-frame. Alternatively, you can press and hold the *Shift* key once you have started moving the end of the clip to override the current snapping setting.

11. Next we need to make the timing of the jumps between Take 1 and Take 2 feel a little more natural by seeing where the changes fall compared to the musical beat or the lyrical phrasing. Don't worry, as this sort of consideration will come naturally to you the more editing you do. To show you what I mean, move your mouse to the middle of the end of the first clip of Take 1 and use the smart tool by clicking and dragging to the right to make the clip a fraction longer. If you lengthen it to the timeline point 00:01:48:05 and play the clip, you will see that the scene change happens at the end of the lyrics "Let's just get on" with the lyric "and go" being on Take 2. This certainly feels much more of a musical edit. In the same manner, move the beginning of the second clip on Take 1 to 00:02:01:00 and we will achieve the same musical kind of edit. You can even add a slight fade offset to the beginning of the second clip that is about five frames long. By moving the mouse to the top-left corner of the clip, the fade icon will appear allowing you to add the fade in, which will make Take 2 feel even smoother as it fades back to Take 1. As you increase or decrease your fade time, Vegas will show the changes numerically in the number of frames on the **Fade Offset Display** shown in the next screenshot:

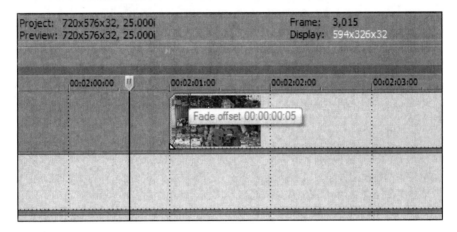

What just happened?

Firstly we saved our project at the same point of editing as two separate projects called "Video Tutorial" and "Multicamera". This was done so that we can explore two different methods of "Editing" or "Cutting" our media clips to create a smooth flowing and engaging music video clip. Working on our Video Tutorial we began the first method by going on to identify an area in Take 1 that needed to be removed from the useful pool of footage, and separated and deleted this piece of media from the timeline using Split and Delete commands. Once removed we fine tuned the edit to make the changes from Take 1 and Take 2 feel smoother and more musical. You are on your way to possibly being that Academy Award Winning Editor!

Have a go hero – finding glitches and unwanted video artefacts

I want you to now go through Take 1 and Take 2 individually to find any glitches or events that you feel need to be removed from the media. Follow the same format and method as we have just used in the previous *Time for action* section. You can compare your edits with mine later on. Remember, we are looking for actual errors or glitches, not personal creative choices. Those other creative choices can come later. Leave Take 3 for the moment as it is a different kind of track. Make sure you save your project when you have finished editing.

Method two: Multicamera tool

Previously we used a manual way to edit our media for the music video clip, but within the arsenal of Vegas Pro 11 there is a very powerful and useful tool called the Multicamera Tool. This tool is ideal for the purposes we are currently dealing with in our music video. That is multiple takes of a similar event that we wish to choose and cut from. Be aware that this process is a lot more CPU intensive, so if the video preview becomes choppy or stuttered, then lower your preview monitor quality to **Preview** or even **Draft** so that the timing of the cuts will be more accurate. Dependent upon your computer power you may have to forego video quality over timing while editing. Let's go through the process now.

Time for action – creating edits with the Multicamera tool

You will recall that earlier we saved two version of our project. Now is the time to save and close the one you've been working on and open up the Multicamera project.

If you saved correctly, upon opening Multicamera, you should see the three complete video tracks called Take 1, Take 2, and Take 3 plus one audio track called Master Audio.

1. We now turn on Multicamera editing by choosing from the menu **Tools | Multicamera | Enable Multicamera Editing** or pressing the keys *Ctrl + Shift + D*. You will see that a blue border appears around the preview monitor.

2. While holding the *Ctrl* key, select each Track header for the video tracks until all three are highlighted as in the following screenshot:

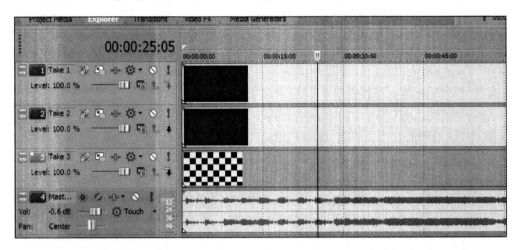

3. Please ensure the Tracks are named Take 1, Take 2, and Take 3 as this is an essential part of the Multicamera process. Once they are named correctly, select **Tools | Multicamera | Create Multicamera Track**. You will see two things happen. Firstly, it will appear that you only have one video track now, but the preview monitor is cut into four sections and you will see that they have taken on the names of the track. The fourth box is black as we only had three active video tracks. See the following screenshot:

4. The currently active take has the blue box around it. That is, the take that has the blue box is the take that will have priority at that point in the timeline and until another selection is made. Although there only appears to be one video track on our timeline, all three video tracks are in fact stacked on top of each other ready for our selection. The selection process is an easy one and everything we do here is undoable and/or editable.

5. Let's take the timeline back to the beginning and press the *space bar* to start play back. Watch the preview monitor and you will see that Takes 1 and 2 are continuous performances, but Take 3 is a series of media clips that are separated by a checkerboard background. First thing we will do is remove the checkerboard background from the take.

6. Take the timeline back to the beginning again (using the *Ctrl + Home* keys on your keyboard as a shortcut, or the *W* key). Now by using the right-hand arrow key on your keyboard, you can nudge the timeline along in increments of around three frames, which is a default setting dependent upon your level of zoom on the timeline. If, for example, you were zoomed in closer on the timeline, the increments would drop to two frames or one frame accordingly. Keep pressing the right-hand arrow key until the first video of the guitar player appears in the Take 3 quarter of our preview monitor. Once you see it, use the *Alt* key and the Left and Right arrow keys to move the timeline in one frame increments back and forward until you find the very first frame of the guitar player in Take 3. Once there, click your mouse in the middle of the Take 3 window on the preview monitor:

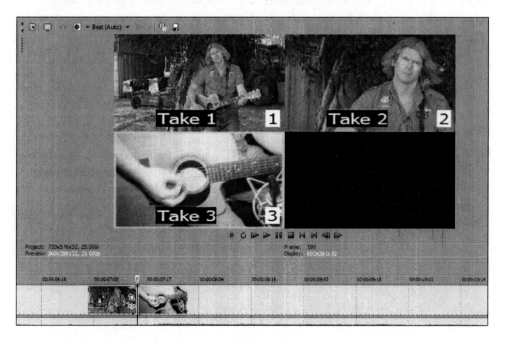

7. As you can see, the blue box has now moved around the Take 3 window and on the timeline a split point has been made on our media. With a closer look you will now see that the left-hand side of the split point is Take 1 and the right-hand side is Take 3. Continue to nudge the timeline along until you find the end of the guitar player in Take 3 by pressing the right arrow key and then pressing the *Alt + Right/ Left* arrow keys to find the last frame. That is just before the checker background appears again. Now, click on Take 1 again.

8. Take the timeline back to the beginning (press the *Ctrl + Home* keys as long as the whole project length is visible) and push play and you will see that the blue box now automatically jumps from Take 1 to Take 3 and back again at the appropriate points.

9. Your task now is to go through the above process and create split points for the remaining 18 clips of footage on Take 3. You can compare your results when all are done with the following screenshot:

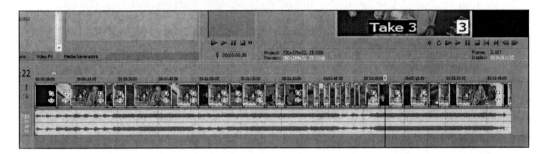

10. Now that we have divided up Take 3, we can add some Take 2 into the mix. We could go through and add more split points to the edit, or we have the ability to make some adjustments to the existing ones. The first scene we currently see is the long shot of our singer, followed by a studio shot of the guitarist, and then back to the long shot. I think it would be nice to have the first time we see him actually sing to be a closer shot. To do this we right-click in the middle of the third media clip we have created and select **Take** from the drop-down menu. In here, at the bottom you will see Take 1, Take 2, and Take 3 displayed with a little circle next to Take 1. Let's change this to Take 2. Now our third shot in the sequence is a closer shot taken from Take 2.

11. If you remember our previous method, we removed the crew member that stepped in and fixed the singer's hair. Once again we will need to do this, and we can by changing the scenes that contain the crew member to Take 2. Let's do this now.

12. The first clip we need to change to Take 2 is the media clip that has its left hand edge at 00:01:49:12 on the timeline. Just as before, right-click in the middle of this clip, select **Take**, and change to Take 2. Do the same to the three clips starting at 00:01:53:04, 00:01:56:15, and 00:02:00:18 accordingly. This removes the random crew member from the clip. Now that you have this method down, go through and make changes to the other Take 1 clips that you feel are good options as well as use this method to remove any other unwanted scenes, glitches, and so on, from the video. It is best to leave the Take 3 scenes as they are as we will be referencing them further along in the tutorial.

13. Another quick way to get the split points close to the mark is to start the timeline from the beginning, hit play, and as the video travels along in real time make the selections on the preview monitor. To do this, click on the take you would like to be active at that point in time, like doing a Live Camera Switch during a football match or the shooting of a TV soap opera. Once done you can come back and edit the selection's start and finish times. This process takes a little more skill and familiarity with the footage at hand but, once your editing skills improve, this will seem like a logical step for you to do.

14. To finalize the Multicamera session, select from the menu **Tools | Multicamera | Expand to Multiple Tracks**. It will offer you an option **Keep unused takes as muted events (to enable later recombining**?). Select **Yes** for now, but as you become more confident and you are sure there are no more edits you can select **No** to remove the unwanted media clips from the timeline. After selecting Yes, the expanded tracks will now still contain all the media clips with the un-chosen clips being grayed out or muted, and the active clips being lighter and active. Now take the timeline to the beginning, hit play, and watch the preview monitor to see our work in action. To remove the blue border and the Take number, go to **Tools | Multicamera** and uncheck **Enable Multicamera editing** or press *Ctrl + Shift + D*. This takes the system out of Multicamera edit mode.

What just happened?

Using the Multicamera tool as our second method of editing, we were able to make various creative and essential selections from our three takes to create a flowing and cohesive music video clip. One of the beauties of non linear or digital editing is that you aren't actually cutting film up into little pieces, which means nothing we do here is permanent. We can make decisions later into the project or even at the last minute that would have been impossible in the old days of film editing. The Undo button (*Ctrl + Z*) is certainly our friend!

Event panning and cropping tool

Earlier in the book we made mention of the two icons that appear at the right-hand end of each media clip. Here, we will look at the Event Pan/Crop tool that one of these icons represents and has been circled in the following screenshot:

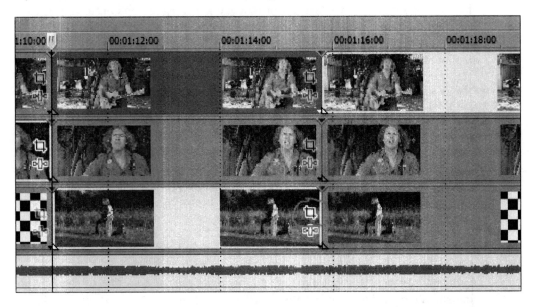

Clicking on this icon will open up the Panning and Crop window with the selected clip loaded into the workspace ready to work on. We will use this tool to achieve two things. First, we will create a zoom-in effect on a clip and then we will remove some unwanted objects from a clip as well.

Panning is the result of moving the camera slowly from one side to the other; particularly for wide landscape shots or moving from one face to the other. It can also be used to bring the focus to one particular part of a scene by zooming and panning onto that spot. Usually this effect is done in the camera at the time of shooting, but this tool allows the editor to add some creative post-camera work. This effect is also commonly used on still images to create a sense of movement. Rather than just showing a series of photographs, each photo is panned across it to take away the static feeling of the still images. This same method applies to moving clips that are in themselves a fairly still image. Let's give it a go now.

Time for action – making a creative zoom with the Pan/Crop tool

Post production digital pan and zoom is a very useful editing tool which gives our project that professional look and feel. Let's apply them to our music video clip.

1. The media clip we will be dealing with is the shot of the singer sitting on his luggage at the side of the road on the timeline at 00:01:11:00 from Take 3. Go to this clip and click on the **Event Pan/Crop** tool icon on the right-hand end of this clip.

2. A new window will open showing a still from the media clip with a letter **F** over it in a bounding box with eight adjustable boxes around it. You will notice below the frame a timeline with a track header that says **Position** and below that **Mask**. We will be dealing with the Position track. This timeline represents the duration of the selected media clip, which in this case is about 00:00:04:20 in length:

3. Now by clicking on the timeline within the Event Pan/Crop window at around three seconds in, you will see that the image in the frame updates to the event at that time. You will notice that the character waiting is looking at his watch. As the lyric of the songs says *Please don't make me wait here forever* at this point, it would be good to bring the viewers attention to this moment.

4. With the cursor sitting at the 00:00:03:00 mark in the **Event Pan/Crop** window, activate the sync cursor icon which is highlighted in yellow in the next screenshot:

5. Grab the top-right adjustment tab of the frame and move it towards the center of the image. If you can still see your preview monitor, you will notice the zooming in effect we are creating, and also that a small diamond has appeared on the position track in the **Event Pan/Crop** window timeline at the point the cursor is sitting at. You will also note that there is one at the very beginning of the timeline. These two diamonds represent the two positions of the Pan / Crop frame. One for the start position and one for the end position. Multiple points are allowable where you can move the Pan / Crop boxes multiple times and positions within a clip.

6. If you right-click directly onto one of the diamonds, you will see they have a variety of settings such as Cut, Copy, Paste, Linear, Fast, Slow, Smooth, and so on. If you change both our diamonds to **Smooth**, in our example you will see the zoom now feels even more like an actual in-camera zoom. Alternatively, if you set the first diamond to **Hold**, the frame won't move from its first position until it reaches the second diamond and there it will quickly jump to the second position. All these options are creative tools that you can explore at your leisure to see how they affect your edits.

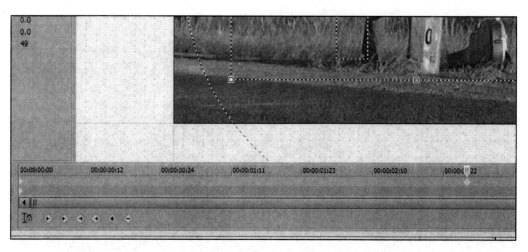

7. Close or dock the Event Pan/Crop window and make sure you can see the preview monitor. Click the cursor just to the left of the media clip we have been dealing with on the main timeline and hit play. Now you will see the panning / zooming effect we just created. The speed of this zoom is editable by simply clicking on the right-hand diamond and sliding to the left to speed up the zoom or to the right to slow it down.

8. Also, one thing we have to be conscious of in doing this is the quality of the media clip. As we zoom in we are in effect reducing the number of pixels that are being used to display the image, so if we zoom in too far on a low resolution image it will start to show up as grainy or jagged edge footage. As you deal with higher quality HD footage in your projects, the amount of zoom allowable increases dramatically.

Time for more action – removing an unwanted shadow

There are two clips in this video with a shadow of the camera man in them that we want to remove. The Event Pan/Crop tool allows us to do this very effectively. Let's try it now.

1. The clips are on Take 3 at 00:01:47:08 and 00:01:54:20. Place your cursor at the first timeline number. In the preview monitor you will notice the scene of the man picking up his guitar and bag to get into the car and on the right-hand side of the scene the cameraman's shadow is visible:

2. Click on the **Pan/Crop** icon for that media clip and as before drag the middle right-hand adjustment bar towards the middle of the scene until the shadow is not visible in the preview. It won't need a lot of movement until it is gone. Play the video to make sure you are happy with the result and that the shadow is now gone:

3. Now because we are going to apply the same cropping to the second scene we can save ourselves a little time by saving this setting and re-applying it with one click of the mouse. In the **Event Pan/Crop** window, you will see at the very top of the frame a preset drop-down menu that has the word (**Untitled**) in it. At the right-hand end there is a symbol of a floppy disk that allows us to save our settings. Highlight the word (Untitled) and rename the setting. A name such as "Take 3 shadow remove" would be a good description for the preset. Once you have typed your Preset Name, click on the floppy disk icon. Now click the down arrow just to the left of the floppy icon and check that your setting name is there at the bottom of the list.

4. Click the **Pan/Crop** icon on the media clip that starts at 00:01:54:20. You will see it's the same scene, but the man is now at the car about to close the back door after putting his bags in. Select the down arrow of the drop down Preset menu and select the preset "Take 3 shadow remove" that you saved previously. Instantly the crop frame will move into the correct position. We have now removed the cameraman's shadow from the scenes we have used as seen in the next screenshot:

What just happened?

The Event Pan / Crop tool is a very powerful tool that is only limited by your imagination. We have learned how to crop a scene to remove unwanted content as well as learning the basics of automating the tool. This method of automation like we set up in the Scene Zoom applies to pretty much every plugin and tool within Vegas Pro 11. Make sure you have a good grasp of this process before proceeding, and especially the adding of points to the position timeline within the Event Pan / Crop tool. For more information and another tutorial have a look at the *How to Crop, Scale and Rotate Video* interactive tutorial found under the **Help Menu | Interactive Tutorials** of Vegas pro 11.

Slow and fast motion

The last thing we will look at in this chapter is slow and fast motion. Slowmo as it is often referred to, is a much used tool in the creative process. It is also a standard tool in the sporting world to slow the film down to see that special moment in the game or competition. We have all seen it before, and enjoyed the **Slow Motion** effect. Its half brother **Fast Motion** isn't used nearly as much, but has been a favorite in comedy and many older films to speed up the story line, get to the point more quickly, or to give a feeling of intense hustle and bustle. In the film world this used to be achieved by making the film go through the camera at a much faster rate like 50 frames per second while being filmed, then once processed it would be played back at 24 frames per second making the action pass by the projector lens slower than was filmed. Likewise for fast motion, the film was shot at a lower frame rate and then sped up again in the play back. There was a fair bit of fiddling and mathematics going on to get the right look, but today with digital processing this is a very easy effect to achieve.

Time for action – using slow motion as a creative tool

Slow and fast motion effects are great creative tools, which we will now use on our project.

1. Let's apply a little slowmo to one of our media clips for a little creative input. Obviously we won't be applying it to a part where he is singing as this would throw out the lip sync. So let's apply it to one of our story telling clips. Let's jump to the media clip on Take 3 at 00:00:32:18. It's the clip where the red car flies past and our character is sitting on his suitcase waiting and throwing a rock.

2. Firstly, let's remove the clip directly after the clip in question. Click on the clip on Take 3 that starts at 00:00:36:03, the one directly after the clip we are applying slowmo to, and press *Delete* on your keyboard (or *Ctrl + X*). Now we have some room to move.

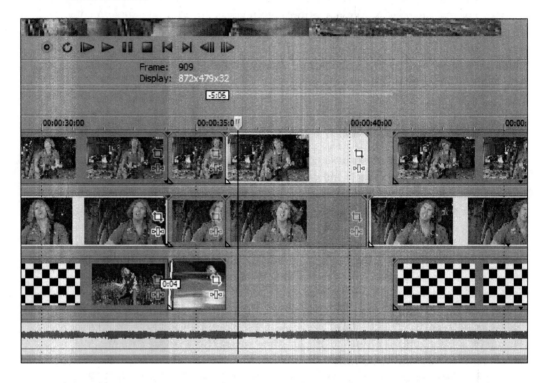

3. Using the smart tool that we would normally use to lengthen the media clip, place your mouse at the center at the end of our clip. While holding the *Ctrl* button click the mouse in the middle of the end of the clip. You will notice the **Lengthening** icon appears, but with a squiggly line under it. We are now ready to make the clip travel in slow motion. While continuing to hold the *Ctrl* button, drag the mouse to the right about 50 frames or 2 seconds if you like (50 frames is 2 seconds in PAL).

4. Click anywhere to the left of our edited clip and hit play. You will see our character is now in a slow motion state. We haven't changed the duration or timing length of the clip, but have simply made the clip show us less frames within the time allotted. This is much easier than slowing down cogs and pulleys in a projector!

5. To put the clip into Fast Motion we would do exactly the same thing except pull the end of the clip towards the front of the clip. This would in turn make more frames pass by in the allotted time to make it speed up in playback.

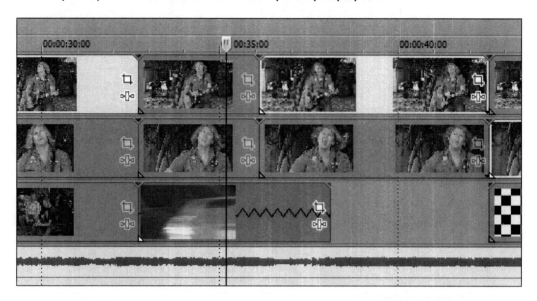

6. You will also notice, as in the previous image, that a jagged or squiggly line appears through the centre of the clip to let us know it has been slowed down (or sped up). Have a fiddle with a few of the clips if you wish that aren't reliant on lip sync or music playback timing and you can add a little creative flare to some of the action shots. Save the project at this point before you start to experiment so you can come back to this, our working version, if you make a mistake.

Pop quiz

1. To make an Edit or Split point to a media clip, we use the key combination?

    a. *Ctrl + F*

    b. *Ctrl + K*

    c. *Ctrl + E*

    d. *Ctrl + S*

    e. The *S* key on its own

2. To remove an unwanted piece of a media clip that has been cut from the timeline we use?

    a. *Ctrl + X*

    b. The *Delete* Key

    c. *Ctrl + V*

    d. *Ctrl + Q*

3. Which tool has to be enabled to have all three Takes visible on your preview monitor at the same time?

    a. The Slow Motion tool

    b. The Event Pan / Crop tool

    c. The Enable Multicamera Editing tool

4. In Vegas Pro 11, zooming in on a subject in a scene is done by using?

    a. The Zoom button on my camera

    b. The Zoom tool

    c. The Event Pan / Crop tool

    d. You can't do it in Vegas Pro 11

5. Slow Motion or slowmo is achieved by?

    a. Making the actor go slow

    b. Putting your finger on the cogs of the Projector

    c. Using the Smart tool while holding down the *CTRL* button

    d. Right-click the clip and select *Slow Motion*

Summary

We learned a lot in this chapter about the history of editing and cutting film. Although not necessary, there are many books and articles on the methods used by different editors who are willing to give away their secrets.

Also we looked at two of the different methods used for editing or cutting together a film clip or series of takes.

- ◆ Method 1: Using the Split tool and creating cuts in specific places in the media clip
- ◆ Method 2. Using the Multicamera tool to switch between takes both in real time and manually

The Event Pan / Crop tool is a powerful tool as we have seen that can be valuable to both the Creative and Media Maintenance processes. Slow and Fast motion is now an easy thing to achieve in the Digital world.

Having whetted your appetite even further towards your goal of Academy Award Winning editor, let's now take this new found confidence and delve even further into the mystical art of Editing in our next chapter.

4
Essential Editing Tools

Vegas Pro 11 has an abundance of editing tools under the bonnet. This chapter will continue to take us along the path to learning how to use and apply these tools and will help bring you closer to being the Editor you want to be.

In this chapter, we shall look at:

- ◆ Video effects (a.k.a. FX)
- ◆ FX globally and individually
- ◆ Transitions
- ◆ Media generators
- ◆ The advent of 3D editing

So let's get on with it...

Important preliminary points

We shall continue to edit our music video clip. Even though some of these tools will not be used in the final version of the music video clip, by using this media we will have a better understanding of the power of the software.

Video effects (a.k.a. FX)

The palette of video effects that we have at our fingertips allows us to make changes to the look and feel of our Media that, before digital editing, may have taken hours to achieve. But today, the results can be seen with the click of a button or preset.

With over 57 FX that come standard with Vegas Pro 11, we won't be covering every one in this book. But the methods we will use to change and save settings, automate and change parameters, and in general manipulate the FX in our music video clip, applies to them all.

Time for action – applying global FX to our media

If it isn't already, open up our Video Tutorial project so we can continue to edit it. So far we have used the Multicamera tool to create a satisfying compilation of the three video tracks. Now that we have this edit, we need to address the footage in both a corrective and creative manner. We shall first look at the Creative point of view and in the process learn how to generally apply FX to our project.

Track 3 is a series of scenes that aren't necessarily relevant to the timeline of the *video* story, so they are in effect a different *time* in the history of the song. To keep this separated from the performance of the song, we shall *desaturate* the footage to give it an almost Black and White feel, but leaving some color. This will make these scenes feel as if they are from a different time than the rest of the performance footage:

1. Place the cursor on the timeline at 00.00.26.00. The preview should be showing the scene of the three boys in the band sitting in the studio having a laugh.

2. Click the **VIDEO FX** tab or use the keys *ALT + 8*.

3. Locate the **Saturation Adjust** plugin, and click and drag it onto the **Track FX** button of Track 3.

4. The **Video Track FX** window will open and you will see that the plugin settings are available. Move the **Center** setting all the way to the left at **0**. The same with **Spread** to the left till **0.0100**, and lastly move the **High** setting to the left to **-0.8200**.

5. Close the **Video Track FX** window:

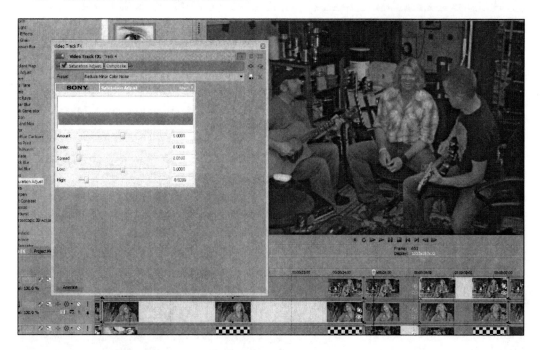

What just happened?

From the menu of the available Video FX, we selected the **Saturation Adjust** plugin. By clicking and dragging this *effect* onto the **Video FX** button of Track 3, we applied this effect to all of the video that lays on Track 3. This is also known as globally applying an effect to the track. If you look at the previous screenshot, you can see that in the **Video Track FX** window, there is a black tick mark next to the **Saturation Adjust** tab at the top. By clicking this, you can turn the plugin on and off.

Here we have learned how to apply Video FX to a track. This can apply to pretty much all of the FX in the Video FX window. Obviously, the creative choices are endless as well as the combination of parameters within each plugin. By trying a few different FX on Track 3 you can see for yourself some of the options available.

Have a go hero – doing more with the FX

Switch off the Saturation Adjust effect and go through each of the FX that interests you and apply them to Track 3. You can adjust the parameters manually, or if you prefer select a preset from the drop-down menu to see how those effects look. After inserting each effect, you will need to remove each plugin before applying the next one. This can be done by selecting the plugin (in blue) and clicking on the **Remove Selected Plug-in** button just to the right of the listed plugins. Hovering over this icon will reveal the function name. Make sure the timeline is set to view one of the scenes on Track 3:

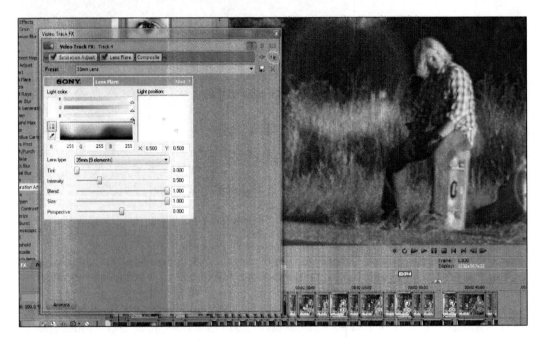

Global FX (another option)

Another way to add a Video FX to a clip globally is to right-click in the middle of a media clip and from the list select **Media FX**. Now the Media FX window will open allowing you to add the FX of your choice to edit or select as a preset. Now, any time a section of that clip appears active, it will have the selected FX applied.

Time for action – applying FX to individual clips

Similar to the previous section, we can add FX to individual clips when needed. Continuing to edit our Track 3, we want to make the story telling scenes of the track slightly different to the studio scenes. With this in mind, let's add a different look to those scenes to give the impression of a special time, possibly in the past.

1. The first scene that is story telling on track 3 is the clip starting at 00:00:32:18. Place the cursor in the middle of this clip on Track 3. (This is the first time you see Dane sitting on his suitcase).

2. From the **Video FX** window find the **Starburst** plugin and click/drag it onto the clip. The **Video Event FX** window will open again with the **Starburst** plugin active.

3. From the drop-down preset window select **Simple 4 Point**, and then in the parameter window, change the **Threshold** setting to **89.25**. You can either use the slider or double-click on the numeric value to type in the number you want.

4. You will see in the preview window that the scene now has a starburst effect across certain highlights in the scene.

What just happened?

We have now learned how to apply FX to individual media clips. You can keep adding FX to the same clip if that creates the look you are after, but of course the ability of the computer to play back all of the FX in real time becomes harder as the number of FX increases. Also the power of your CPU will be a discerning factor.

Have a go hero – doing more with the Media FX

There are eight clips on Track 3, which make up the story telling section of the clip containing Dane waiting and or getting into the car. I want you to now apply the same effect to the remaining seven clips, using the process we just applied. Remember, to speed things up you can save the preset of the first setting with the **Threshold** at **89.25**, and give it a name you can remember. You can then simply select it again from the preset drop-down list once the FX is on the clip.

Also remember to save the project again once you have completed this task.

Before we move on to our next topic, *Transitions*, we need to prepare our project to be able to apply them to our media clips.

Now that we are fairly happy with our edits, it is time to get rid of the unnecessary muted clips on each track and consolidate all of the media clips onto one track.

Time for action – removing the muted media clips

Although we have three tracks active, each edit is switching from one track to another as it comes across each edit. Our goal is to leave the active clip for each edit and remove the two remaining muted clips. Back in the Multicamera edit mode there was a function that does this for you automatically, but by doing it manually here it will give you a better understanding of what the automatic mode is doing for you:

1. From the **View** menu, select the second icon from the bottom called **Minimize All Tracks**. It will look like this:

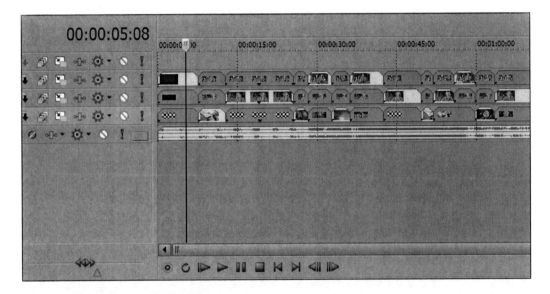

2. You will notice that it has become far easier to see which clips are muted and which are active for each edit. The active clips are highlighted with a white background, whereas the muted clips have a grey background.

3. Click on each grayed-out clip and once highlighted, hit the **Delete** button on your keyboard. Work your way through all the edits until you have one active clip left for each edit. If you have any trouble seeing each individual edit, zoom in on the timeline by either rolling your mouse wheel forward or using the **+** sign in the bottom right hand corner of the timeline.

4. The resulting timeline should look like the following screenshot once zoomed out all the way:

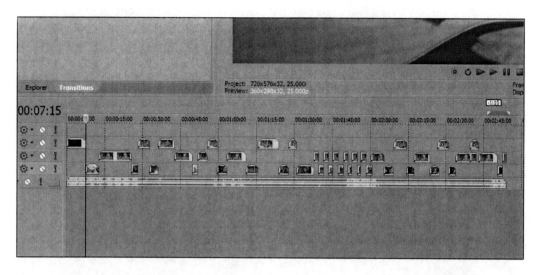

5. You can also go back to the **View** menu and turn off the **Minimize All Tracks** function. The result will look like this:

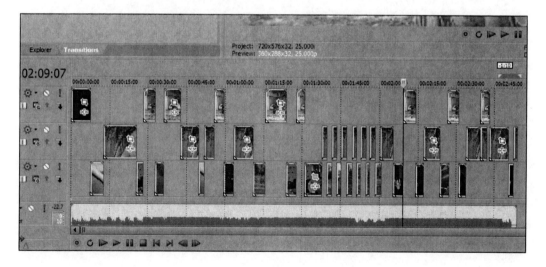

6. From the **Edit** menu, choose the **Selection** tool from the **Editing** tool menu. You will notice that when you place this tool on the timeline, a box appears next to the mouse. This is a Bounding box that allows you to select a group of media clips all at once.

7. On Track 2, place the cursor just in front of the first media clip, hold the left mouse button down, and drag it along Track 2 until all the media clips on Track 2 are selected, then let go. You will notice that the white boundary line around the clips has disappeared to let you know they have been selected. See the following screenshot:

8. Once again from the **Edit** menu and from the **Editing** tool menu choose the **Normal** tool. (These tools can also be accessed from the top of the Vegas main window). Now carefully click and hold the first media clip on Track 2 and slide all the Track 2 clips up onto Track 1. Make sure you don't slide the clips forward or backward on the timeline or your lipsync will be out. If the orange line at the beginning of the first clip stays orange, you know you did slide the clips properly. Once in place with the orange cursor, let go of the mouse button.

9. Right-click in the middle of the now empty Track 2 and select **Delete Track**. Your timeline should look like the following screenshot:

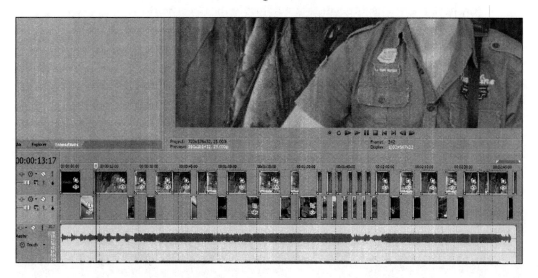

10. We will now do the same operation to Track 3, but before we do that, you will remember that we applied a global Track FX with the **Saturation Adjust** plugin to this track. If we were to slide the clips off of that track then the effect will no longer be applied to the clips. First we need to click on the **Track FX** button of Track 3 so that we can save our Saturation Adjust setting as a preset.

11. Once the **Video Track FX** window is open, click in the **Preset** name pane, call the preset **Track 3**, and hit the Floppy Disk symbol to the right of the name. Then uncheck the tick next to **Saturation Adjust** to turn the FX off:

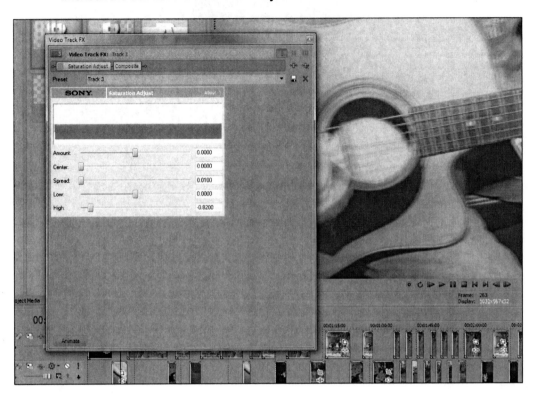

12. Close the rack FX window.

13. Right-click on the first clip on Track 3 and select **Media FX**.

14. From the list that appears choose **Sony Saturation Adjust** and hit the **OK** button at the top-right of the **Plug-In Chooser**.

15. From the **Media FX** window, select from the **Preset** drop-down window the setting called **Track 3** that we saved previously and close the **Media FX** window. We have now applied the Saturation Adjust setting to all of the clips on Track 3.

16. As before, use the selection tool to *Rubber Band* the clips on Track 3 and carefully slide them up onto Track 1, keeping the orange cursor at the beginning of the first clip to ensure no slide happens.

17. Right-click in the middle of the now blank Track 3 and choose **Delete Track**.

What just happened?

We have now cleared all the muted tracks from our project, and have consolidated all of the active media clips onto one track. We can now apply transitions to the changes between the clips. Our Project should now look like the following screenshot:

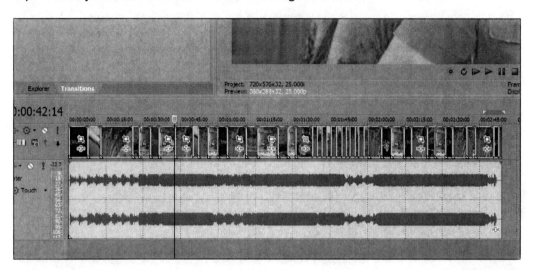

Transitions

As one Media clip stops and the next starts, creating what we have called a cut or edit, it is an instant change. Sometimes this change can call for a smoother or softer switching from one clip to another, and this event is called a **Transition**. Vegas Pro 11 has 24 transitions available as standard with each transition having a wide range of presets available to you. Now that we have all our media clips on one track, we can experiment with and explore how to use transitions.

Time for action – using transitions

Correct use of transitions can make all the difference between an amateur- or professional-looking edit. Let's jump in and learn hands-on how to achieve that professional, finished look.

1. Right-click on the track header of the video track and choose **Expand Track Layers** as shown in the following screenshot:

2. Here you can now see how the media clips alternate between the upper and lower layers of the video track. Using the Smart tool, grab the end of the first clip and drag it out slightly longer so it overlaps the second media clip that is on the lower layer and until the pink line appears. We have now created a transition between clip 1 and clip 2 as can be seen with the white bar between the two clips with the **X** on it. At the moment, the transition is a simple crossfade lasting the default setting of 1 second.

3. Play the clip from just before the transition and see how a crossfade looks.

4. By right-clicking on the transition bar you will see the menu **Fade Type**, and in there a collection of crossfade types. The two crossing lines represent how the first clip fades out as the second clip fades in.

5. Sometimes a crossfade transition is all that is needed, but if you want to get more creative, open the transition window by selecting the **Transition** Tab or using *Alt + 7*.

6. Click and drag the **Cross Effect** transition onto the **Transition** bar between clip 1 and clip 2. The **Video Event FX** window will open showing the available parameters and usual preset window, with the default **Preset Cross Zoom A/B Slow** selected.

7. Play back the video from just before the crossfade and see how it looks. You can see how the video zooms into clip 1 and zooms out of clip 2 to create an effective transition.

8. Now in the Preset window, select **Cross Blur A** only and play back the transition. You can see that the first clip blurs and fades out to reveal the second clip.

9. From the Transition window, click and drag the **Page Peel** transition and drop it onto the Transition bar. It will replace the **Cross Effect** transition with the new one. Play the video again to watch the **Page Peel** transition.

What just happened?

We expanded our Track Layers to reveal the two layers available on our video track. Here we are able to overlap the media clips to create a transition space where we can drag and drop the available transitions as we like. Each transition has many presets available as well as all the parameters we can manually adjust to create a unique setting of our own creation to save as a usable preset.

The main key with transitions is to not have too many different types of transitions in one project, and especially in a music video to keep the transition not too overbearing as they will detract from the content of the music video clip. Also, I would leave most of the edits as clean cuts, and possibly introduce transitions on a few key media clips, such as changing to and from the storytelling scenes back to the performance scenes.

Have a go hero – doing more with transitions

Go ahead and apply a transition to the media clips every time the video changes from the colored performance scenes into the de-saturated storytelling scenes. I would suggest using the **Cross Effect** transition with the preset **Cross Blur B** only. Feel free to experiment with a few of the different transitions, but finish up with the recommended transition. There is probably also no need to use a transition going back from the storytelling to the performance footage, but once again, feel free to experiment with transitions and/ or crossfades. Also take into consideration the length of the crossfades. You will find that sometimes the one second length will feel too long, so just shorten the length of the overlap between the media clips to shorten the transition.

Media generators

Another powerful tool we have access to is the Generated Media tools. Here, we can create Text, Color Gradients, and Pro Type Titling, to mention a few. To show you how we can use these tools, we will create a lower-third title for our music video clip.

Time for action – media generators

If our video was being aired on a music channel, then the addition of the artist's name and song title to a lower-third will take our music video clip into the professional league, ready to broadcast. Let's create that now.

1. Right-click on the **Video Track** header and select **Insert Video Track** (or use *Ctrl + Shift + Q*). You will now have a new video track above our current video track.

2. Right-click in the middle of the new track and select **Insert Generated Media**. The plugin **Chooser** window will open.

3. Select **Sony Color Gradient**. The **Video Media** generator window will open.

4. From the Preset window, select **Fancy Wooden Board** and slide the new media clip all the way to the beginning of the timeline, so it is flush against the Track Header. Also, drag the length of the clip to match the length of the first media clip in our video. See the following screenshot:

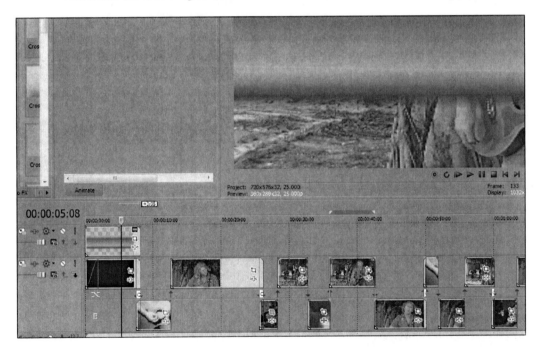

5. You will see that our Orange Wooden Board is proportionately way too big, but we can adjust this. There are three icons on the right-hand side of the generated media clip. Select the middle icon to open the **Event Pan/Crop** window.

6. From the parameters on the left of the **Event Pan/Crop** window, under the **Source** heading, select **Maintain Aspect**, and choose **No** from the drop-down menu.

7. From the **Workspace** heading, change the **Zoom** percentage to around **25%**.

8. Grab the top-left corner of the bounding box and drag it outwards and upwards till the **Position** width is around **2,000** and adjust the position so the Orange wood is near the bottom of the frame. See the following screenshot:

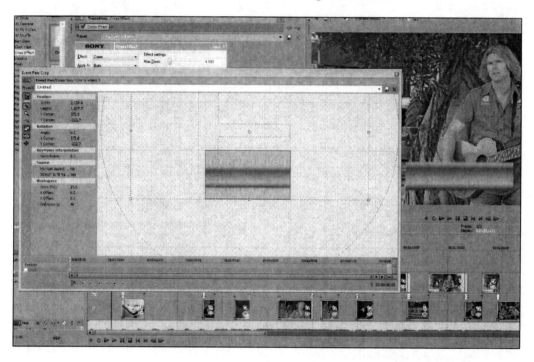

9. While holding down the *Alt* key, grab the middle side bounding box handles and maneuver the frame sides inward. Then adjust the top and bottom outwards till you end up with a shape similar to the following screenshot. If unsure, just replicate the parameter numbers in the screenshot:

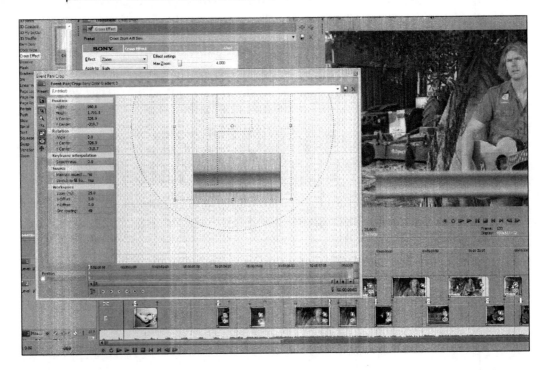

10. One more setting will finish the panel. On the Track Header of the Orange Wooden Panel, select the **Track motion** button, which is on the left of the **Track FX** button. The **Track Motion** window will open. At the very bottom-left corner you will see two check boxes. Tick the **2D Shadow** box to create a drop shadow to complete the floating wooden panel on which we can write our title as shown in the following screenshot:

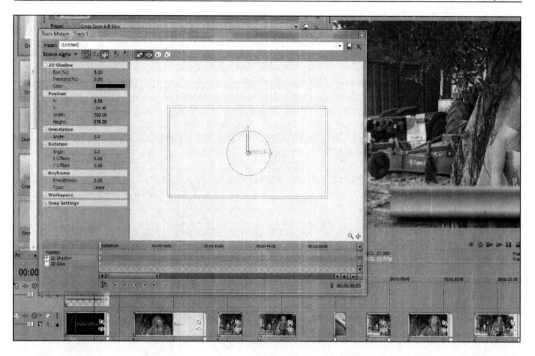

11. Close the **Track Motion** window and use *Ctrl + Shift + Q* to create a new video track above our panel track.

12. Right-click in the middle of our new track and select **Insert Text Media**.

13. In the **Video Media Generator** window, which is now open, highlight the words **Sample Text** so we can type a new heading that will read **Dane Sharp – One way Ride**. Adjust the **Font** size to **36**:

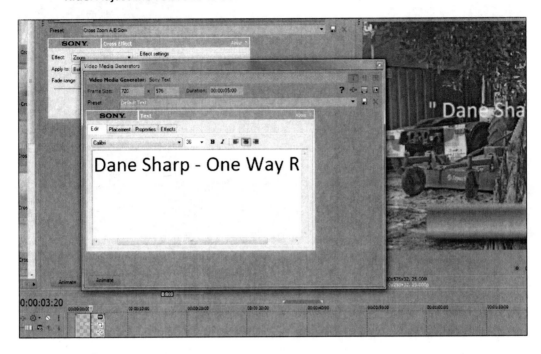

14. Select the **Placement** tab and grab and slide the text till it is floating on our Orange Wooden Panel.

15. Select the **Properties** tab and choose a color that suits the text by clicking on the colored panel or by using the eye dropper next to the colored panel and then using it to select a color from the preview monitor, such as the color of his shirt.

16. Select the **Effects** tab and tick the **Draw Shadow** box to create a drop shadow on the text:

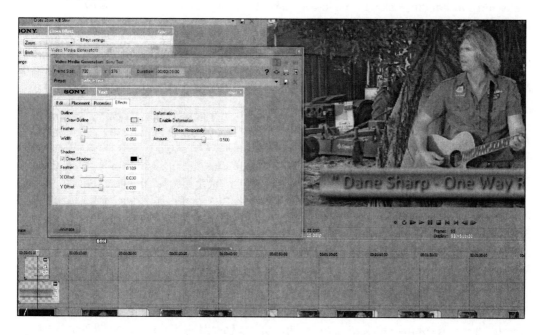

17. Now close the **Video Media Generator** window, and ensure that the Generated Text clip is the same length and position as the Wooden Panel clip on the timeline.

18. Using the Smart tool fade-in and fade-out the Wooden Panel clip, the Text clip, and the first media clip of our music video equally, but leaving the first transition of the music video intact.

19. Now play the video from the beginning and watch the lower-third title do its thing.

What just happened?

We used two types of Media Generators to create a lower-third title for our music video. There are other ways of achieving the same result, such as using the Pro Titler Generator. As you create other opportunities within your projects to use the other media generators, the online tutorials will help you understand them in more detail.

Have a go hero – doing more with media generators

Let's add another dimension to the lower-third title. Have a go at using a transition, such as **Fly In/Fly Out** to make the entry of the lower-third panel and text more interesting. You will need to apply the transition to both media generator clips to make them fly-in together.

The advent of 3D editing

One of the tools available to you in Vegas Pro 11, which certainly makes it stand out from the crowd, is the introduction of 3D editing. Of course, our Tutorial project wasn't shot in 3D and therefore won't be edited in 3D, but all the tools are available for the new craze and production technique that is sweeping the world right now. The beauty is that **3D Editing** or **Stereoscopic Editing**, as it is formally called, doesn't change any of the techniques that we have been looking at so far. The main difference is that your monitoring setup should of course be capable of displaying your video in 3D, so you can see firsthand what you are working on. With all the new 3D cameras that are now becoming available, and the 3D HDTVs that are on the market, you can certainly create you next production in the world of 3D. To enable the 3D editing facility, simply turn on the **Stereoscopic 3D** mode in **Project Properties**, and select from the drop-down menu the best monitoring option that suits both your 3D footage and your 3D monitoring system.

I would highly recommend viewing the online tutorial available for 3D editing if that is an avenue you wish to pursue. This area of Video Production is currently in an ever changing state of technology and standards, but certainly leads to exciting times if you like living on the cutting edge of video production techniques.

Summary

We have learned a lot more in this chapter about the tools available for editing.

Specifically, we covered video effects, how they can be applied to the creative process, and how to apply the FX both globally and individually per clip.

We learned about transitions and how they can help to create the mood and feel of our music video clip, plus how simple it was to add a lower-third panel and text using the media generators within Vegas Pro 11. Also, we touched on a simple outline of the 3D tools available in this powerful editing package.

All of the editing tools and techniques we have been exposed to in the last two chapters will come together to help us have a creative edge over other editors, which leads us on to how we can utilize more of the tools in a corrective and improving manner in the next chapter.

5
Eye Catching Titles, Text, and Effects

As an aid to our music video clip project, I thought I would touch on some of the other powerful tools available in Sony Vegas Pro 11. These tools and ideas will help to add that professional edge to your projects.

In this chapter, we shall cover:

- Titles and text
- Transitions
- Production values

Titles and text

After creating a great video project, that video is often let down by a bad use of text or titles in the project. There are many third-party "Titler" programs available, but thankfully Vegas Pro 11 has some very powerful titler tools built in. In this section, we will look at how to access these tools and apply them to a project.

Time for action – working with the SONY Pro Type Titler

In the past, the only way to achieve professional titles on your video projects was to purchase a third-party program, but Sony Vegas Pro 11 has its very own extremely powerful Titler built in.

1. Let's start a new project and call it **Titles**. In **Project Properties**, let's use the **HD 1080-50i (1920x1080, 25.000 fps)** template. Once you have created and saved this project, insert a video track, right-click on that video track, and select from the drop-down menu **Insert Generated Media...**:

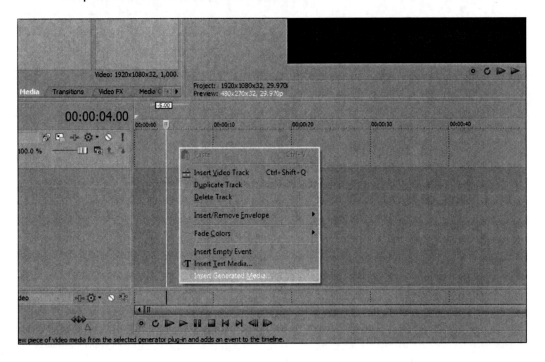

2. The **Plug-In Chooser – New Media Generator** window will now open, and from the list select **Sony Pro Type Titler**:

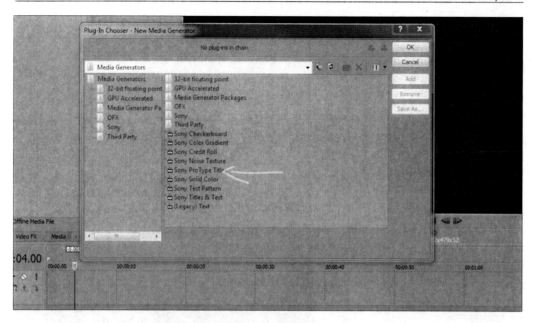

3. Once selected, click **OK** in the Plug-In Chooser window. A new media clip will be placed on the timeline and the **Video Media Generators** window will open showing the parameters for the Sony Pro Type Titler:

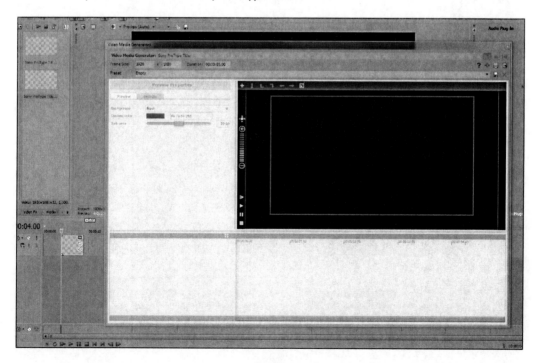

4. The black preview box represents the screen of your project. If you double-click in the black area or click the **+** sign at the top-left corner of the black box, some text will appear with the words **Sample Text**. Also, along the top there is an instruction saying **Text Edit Mode: Click here or press 'Esc' to exit**. This is speaking about exiting the text editing mode of this window:

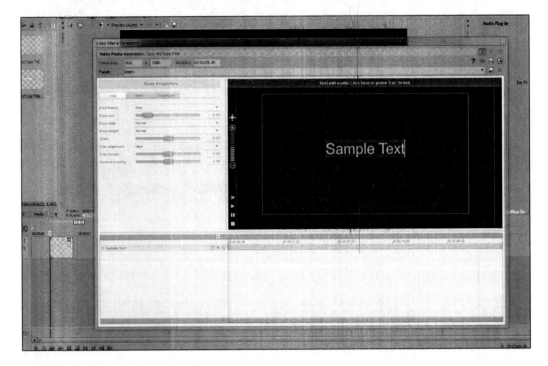

5. The text is highlighted allowing us to type in the words we wish to display. Let's type **Sony Pro Type Titler** for this exercise. If the words **Sample Text** aren't highlighted as in the previous screenshot, use your mouse to select and drag to highlight the words, just as you would in any standard word processing program. Once highlighted, type the new text which will replace the old:

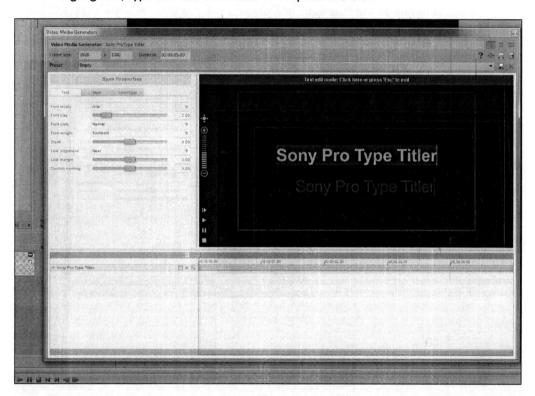

6. Just to the left of the black preview box you will see a selection of the parameters available. The first being **Font family**. If we highlight the words we have just typed, we can select the drop-box arrow next to the word **Arial**. Depending on how many fonts you have on your computer, it may take a few seconds before the drop-down menu appears showing you the fonts available. The good thing about this is as you move your mouse over the fonts, the preview will show you how your text will look in each one. If the preview isn't changing, you must make sure the text is highlighted first. Your font list will look different to mine as I have a very large number of fonts on my system:

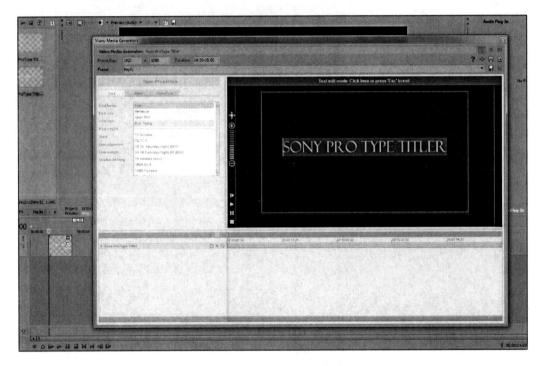

7. The first key to good titles is to select a very clear and readable font. For this exercise, let's go with the font family **Arial** as everyone will have this font on their system. By all means go ahead and look at how all your fonts look before finally selecting the Arial font.

8. The second parameter is **Font size**. Most programs use a point size to define font size, but in this case Sony Pro Type Titler uses a progressive scale ranging from 0.20 up to 10.00 stepping through in two decimal place increments. This method has been chosen as font size in points will vary greatly depending on the *quality* and *size* of your project. For example, using the point size system, if the project was PAL DV, a 10 point font would appear a lot larger on the screen, but would appear quite small on a FULL HD resolution screen. So the font size parameter relates directly to the screen resolution chosen in your Project Properties. By sliding the **Font size** control, you can see how the font will look at different sizes. Alternatively, you can double click the numbers to the right of the Font size slider to type in your preference. The following screenshot shows the Text sized to **3.58**, which fills the screen:

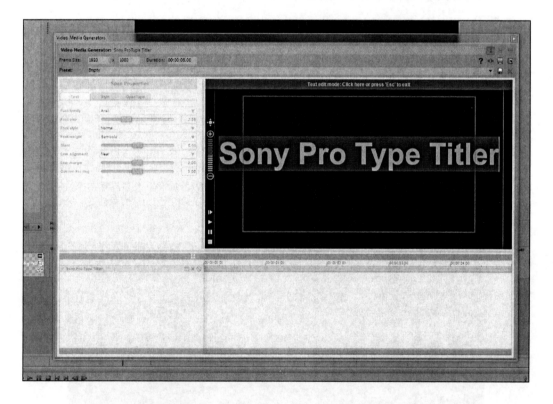

9. Let's return the **Font size** value to **2.00** either by using the slider or typing in the value, so we can continue looking at the other parameters.

10. The options in **Font style** will vary from font to font as this style is dependent upon the variations supplied with the font. Arial has just **Normal** and **Italic** available.

11. **Font weight** is a very useful function. It is like the Bold button on your word processor, but with a lot more variation ranging from **Thin** to **Semibold** to **Extra Heavy** and quite a few variations in between.

12. **Slant** allows us to lean the text either to the left or right; like an Italic setting that we have control over, but also with the ability to slant text to the left. **0.00** keeps the text in its original position while **+** values lean it to the right and **–** values lean it to the left.

13. **Line alignment**: Click the control and choose a setting from the drop-down list to indicate whether you want to align the selected text to the right side (**Near**), **Center**, or left side (**Far**) of the text block.

14. **Line margin**: Drag the slider to set the amount of vertical space lines of selected text. Drag right to increase spacing, or drag left to decrease spacing (low settings will cause lines to overlap or to appear in reverse order). As we have only one line this won't affect our text, but if you wish to experiment hit *Return* at the end of the word Titler and add more words to the second line to see the **Line alignment** in action.

15. **Custom kerning** refers to the distance between letters. The space between certain letters, if the Kerning is equal, can make a word look wrong or out of balance. If you look closely at the letter **T** and **y** in the word **Type** in our heading, you will notice the top of the **T** actually overlaps the beginning of the letter **y**. Without this Kerning setting, the word Type would look incorrect to our eyes. Most fonts automatically adjust their Kerning, but this parameter allows us to make changes to how our words look for an artistic change.

16. Now hit the *Esc* button to exit the edit mode.

What just happened?

We have just seen how to initialize the **Sony Pro Type Titler** and how to enter some text onto the timeline. Next we will look at what we can do with this text.

Time for action – animating our title

Having text on the screen is great and in the old days this was a very hard thing to achieve, but now in the digital world we can not only have text on screen, we can do some very cool things with it.

1. The lower half of our **Video Media Generators** window is allocated to the animation of our title, and Sony has also included some very cool FX collections to use.

2. Just near the bottom left corner of the Preview Screen in the Pro Type Titler, you will see a little icon that is four small boxes forming a square. See it circled in next screenshot:

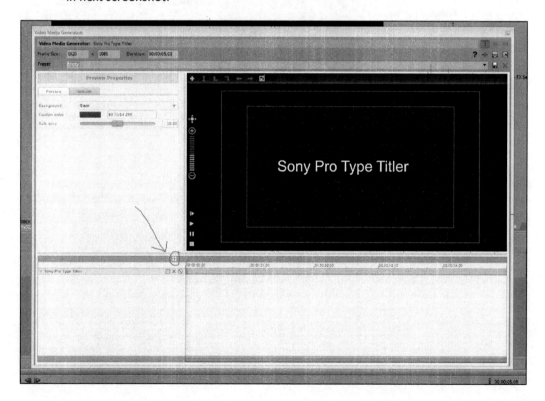

3. Click on this icon once and a list of Collections will appear. Find **Drop split** under **Collections** and double-click it:

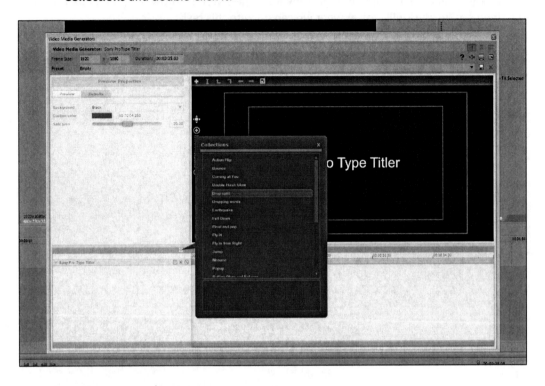

4. You will notice that a bunch of parameters will appear in the lower-half of the **Sony Pro Type Titler** window. The left-hand side is the parameter and the right-hand side is a timeline for that parameter:

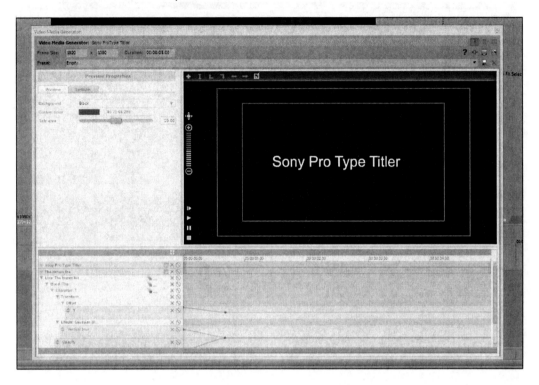

5. If you now press the *spacebar* and watch the preview screen, you will see the words **The brown fox** animate onto the screen. The words drop one-by-one and then once settled they expand and split off of the screen.

6. To make this effect happen to our Title we need to replace the words **The brown fox** with our title.

7. First, let's delete our original title by hitting *Esc* to exit the edit mode and then right-click on the words **Sony Pro Type Titler** and select **Delete**.

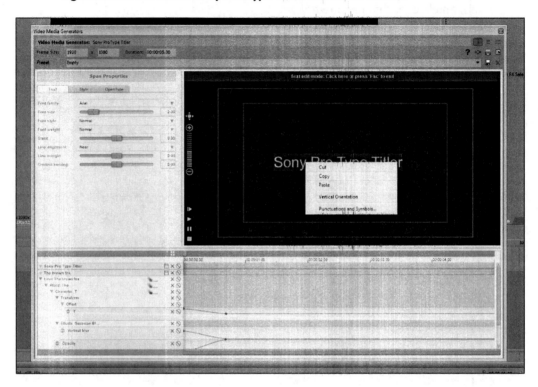

8. In the animation timeline, click your mouse close to the **00:00:02:00** mark to move the cursor to that point. You will see the words **The brown fox** appear. Double-click on the word **brown** to edit the title and highlight all three words:

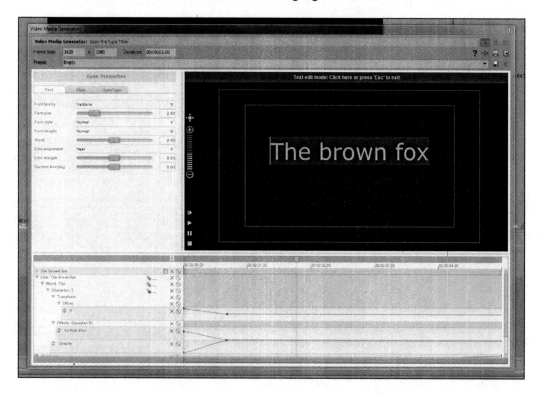

9. Now type our new title to replace the words **The brown fox** with **Sony Pro Type Titler** and hit *Esc* to exit the Text edit mode.

10. Move the animation cursor back to the left at **00:00:00:00** and hit the *spacebar* or use the playback controls circled in yellow in the next image to watch the animation applied to our new title:

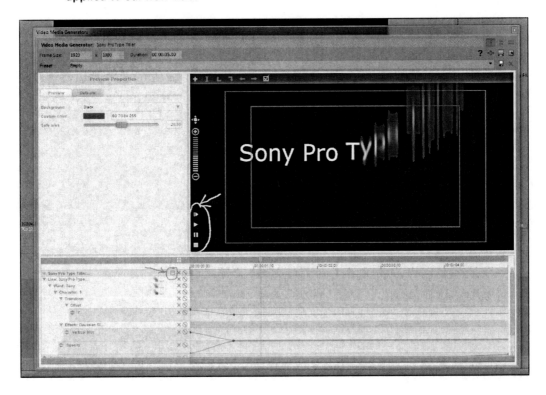

11. You can experiment with the other Collections to see what options you have for creating titles. You can also use the Collections as a starting point and by editing the Parameters on the Animation timeline, you can adjust the collection's settings to better suit your project. These adjustments can also be saved into the Collections list by clicking the Floppy Disk Save icon circled in red in the previous Image.

What just happened?

Using the built-in Sony Pro Type Titler, we were able to create a very professional looking title with animations. These titles are often the difference between an amateur looking project and a professional job.

Creating opening or closing titles

Now that we have created a look for our title, it is easy to continue this process to end up with a series of opening or closing credits.

Time for action – making a series of credits with the Sony Pro Type Titler

Credits are an essential part of a project to satisfy the curious viewer as to who was involved in the creative process. Let's learn how to make those credits look the part.

1. If we were creating a series of text such as opening or closing credits on a project, we could simply copy our media clip on the timeline and just change the words on the second media clip. Let's do that now.

2. Right-click on our media clip on the timeline and select **Copy**.

3. Move the cursor just past our media clip, right-click, and select **Paste**. A **Paste Options** box will appear as shown in the next screenshot:

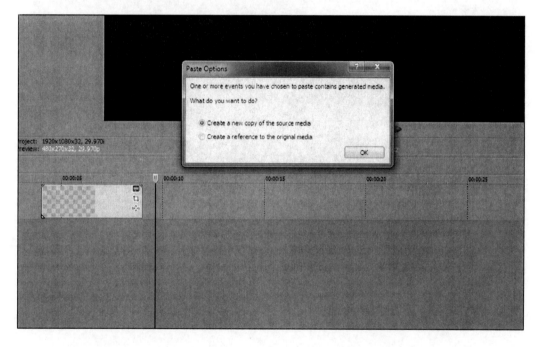

4. As we will be changing the text completely, we want to choose the **Create a new copy of the source media** option.

5. Click the generated media icon at the top-right of the new media clip and the Sony Pro type Titler will open again.

6. Move the animation timeline along close to the **00:00:02:00** mark, so we can see the text and enter the edit Text mode by double-clicking on the words. Highlight and replace the text with the words **Is Awesome**:

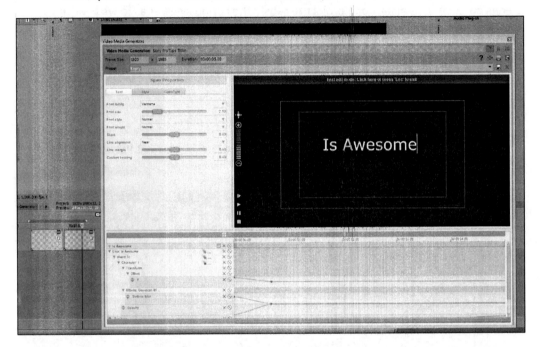

7. Hit *Esc* to exit the Text edit mode and close the Video Media Generators window.

8. If we hit play on our main timeline, we will see that the two media clips bring their text in one after the other. This track could be floating over a colored background or over the opening footage of our project. Thus, creating our opening or closing credits with a creative flair, as in our next image where we used the media generator to create a blue to black color gradient background behind the text.

9. The color gradient background is easily created on a video track below the text by right-clicking on the blank track and selecting **Sony Color Gradient** from the **Insert Generated Media** drop-down menu. Once created, lengthen the color gradient clip to match the duration of the text media clip, as in the next screenshot:

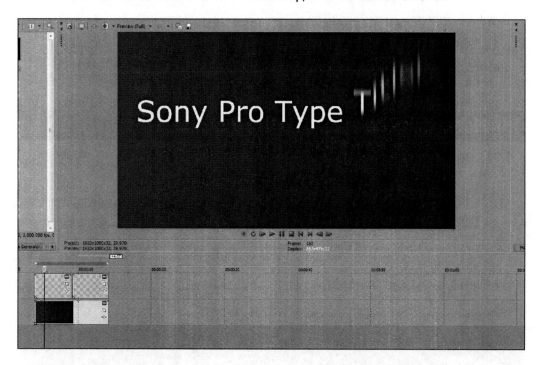

What just happened?

Using the Sony Pro Type Titler and using the Copy Media function we are able to create a professional looking opening or closing credits for our project.

Have a go hero – experimenting with the other Titler Collections

To learn more about the Sony Pro Type Titler, go through the other Collections to see how your text selections respond to the animations. Also try spreading the text across two lines.

Transitions: The key to a smooth flow

The word *Transition* is thrown around the video world but what is it really. The dictionary quotes:

> *TRANSITION: The act of passing from one state or place to the next.*

That is what we are trying to do in a video. Pass from one scene to another, or to give the impression of the same scene passing from one camera view to another, so the transitions you use should be relative to the content and to the emotion.

Time for action – creating effective transitions

A good transition can be the difference between an excellent and average video project. Here we will make yours an excellent one.

1. Let's create a new blank project and call it **Transitions** using the HD 1080-50i (1920x1080, 25.000 fps) template in **Project Settings**.

2. Drag Take 1 and Take 2 from our video clip files onto two video tracks, both starting at 00:00:00:00.

3. Using the *S* key, move the cursor and make four splits on both tracks, and then alternatively remove the media clips, starting with the first clip's second track, so it looks like the following screenshot:

4. Now slide the first two media clips on the bottom track up to the top track:

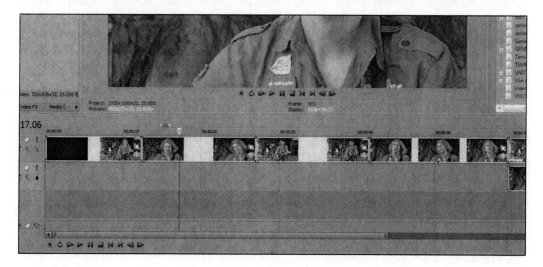

5. The accuracy of our slides isn't important at this stage as we aren't going to worry about bringing the audio in, so we won't have a lip sync problem. For this exercise we are just dealing with the visual aspects of transitions.

6. Now grab the end of the first clip and slide it to the right so that it overlaps onto the second clip. As you slide it, a number will appear between the clips. This is the length of the transition in frames. Once the number reaches **0.25**, it will become **1.00** to represent a one second length:

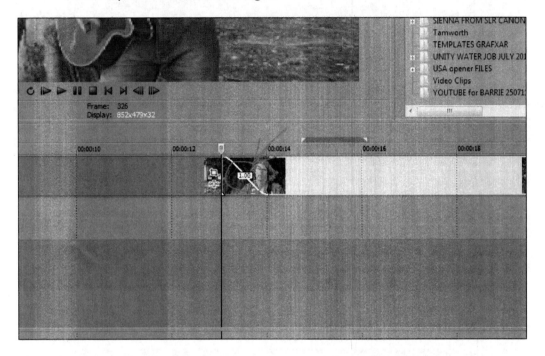

7. This allows us to accurately adjust the length of our transition. At the moment you will see that there is a white line and a blue line creating an **X** through the transition. This indicates that the transition will fade out the first clip and fade in the second. Click just ahead of the transition on the timeline and play the video. You will see the Crossfade transition in action on the Preview Monitor.

8. The first kind of change we can make to the transition is to change the way these two clips fade in and fade out. Right-click in the middle of the crossfade and at the very top of the menu you will see **Fade Type**. Hover your mouse over these words and a selection of different types of crossfades will appear:

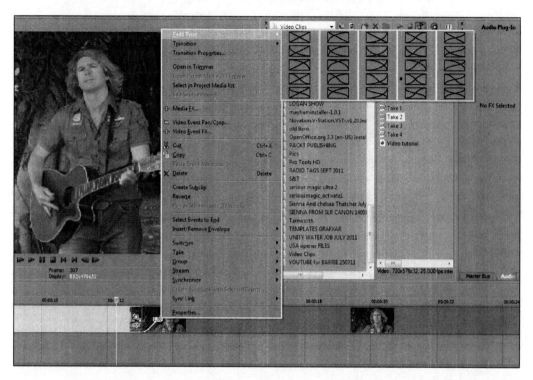

9. The crossfade type with the black dot next to it is the current crossfade. Feel free to try out a few different crossfades to see how it changes the look of the video transition. The differences are subtle, but dependent upon the content of your video, these various crossfades will be perfect for a variety of transition looks.

10. Now we can get a bit more creative with the transitions.

11. Click the **Transitions** tab circled in the next picture to reveal the different transitions available:

12. Click the Transition called **Page Loop** and you will see some variations appear in the right-hand pane. By hovering the mouse over these variations, a small animation will give you an indication of how the transition will affect your footage, with the letter **A** representing the first media clip and **B** the second:

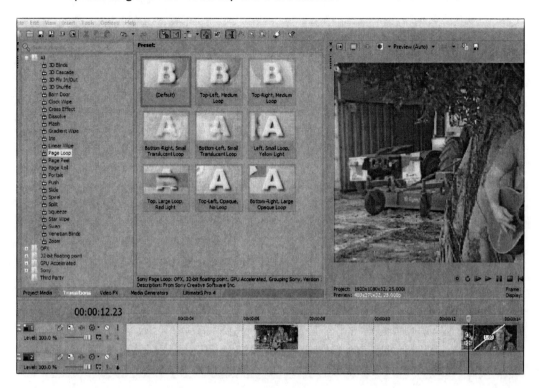

13. Now with your mouse, click and hold the fifth or center transition and drag and drop it onto the crossfade between our two clips. The word **Page Loop** will appear on our transition to verify it has been applied and the parameters for that transition will become available:

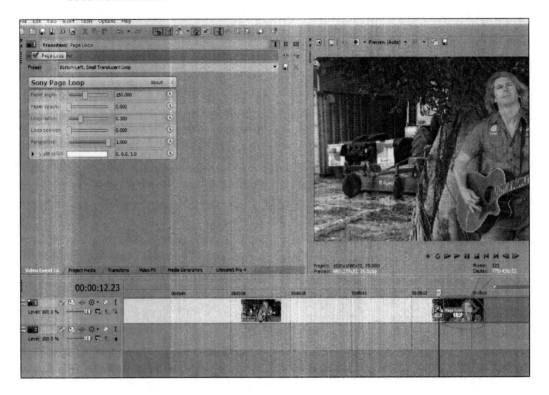

14. Place the mouse before the transition and play the video to watch the transition in action.

15. As with any plugin, there are various presets available for you to experiment with and/or use as a starting point. You can then change the parameters to suit your creative tastes and save as your own uniquely named transitions.

16. To change the transition and to try another style of transition, simply click the **Transitions** tab once again and our list of options will appear. Select the transition you'd like to see. Once you have found one that you like, simply drag and drop the transition over the top of the previous one to replace it.

17. Personally, I rarely use transitions unless I am doing a project that may have a lot of footage that doesn't vary greatly. By using creative transitions, the viewer is stimulated every once in a while by seeing something totally different.

18. For the number of edits in our music video project, having a transition in every cut would be way too much, so limit the use of cuts or short crossfades on your music video project.

What just happened?

We had a look at how to apply transitions to our project. Transitions can be a very useful tool in bringing some life to a video with visually dull content such as a documentary or news bulletin. Go through all of the transitions and see how they look. Remember that certain transitions look so much better dependent on the content of the video clips they are applied to.

Production values

One of the biggest mistakes editors make when creating visuals is to overuse a certain effect, font, transition, or worse still, use way too many in one project. Utilizing good production values is a very important asset to have in your arsenal. Get to know all of the effects, fonts, and transitions you have and what they can do. Being able to visualize your project as you go before you do all the hard work will hold you in good stead to becoming a better professional editor.

Take the time to go through all the **Collections** in the **Sony Pro Type Titler** as well as all of the **Transitions** available to you. Take that extra step and tweak the presets to make them a little more unique to you and your projects, and they can become the very things that make people want to come back to you for your creative talents.

Summary

We learned a lot in this chapter about a few of the extra tools available to you in Sony Vegas Pro 11.

Specifically, we covered:

- How to create titles with the Sony Pro Type Titler: This powerful tool will help to make your project have that professional cinema edge when it comes to text and titles appearing on your project. There is nothing worse than having a great video spoilt by amateur titles.

- Transitions and how they work: Transitions when used sparingly can make a project pop. Add this fantastic tool to your arsenal of go-to effects.

- Production values: Every time you add an effect or process to your workflow or palette, your production value goes up, and this is the key to becoming a better video editor.

Once you have made yourself familiar with the topics discussed in this chapter, let's move forward to the next exciting chapter which will show us how to color correct our music video clip to get it closer to the final render ready for delivery to the client.

6
Color Correction Techniques

The Video Editor is not only a creative being, but also a fixer of problems, as well as an enhancer of the visual product. For one reason or another, such as different cameras, varying lighting during shooting, or a myriad of other reasons, the color of the footage we have to edit doesn't always match from scene to scene. For example, a man's red shirt may look red in one scene but pinker in the next and then possibly purplish in the next.

To help us understand this and other color-related issues, this chapter will cover the following topics:

◆ What are White Balance and Level Correction?
◆ Understanding color correction and how it relates to monitoring and playback
◆ Using the Waveform, Histogram, and other scopes
◆ The Color Correction tool
◆ The Color Corrector Secondary plugin

So let's get on with it...

A note on our project

As always we shall continue to use our music video clip to become accustomed to these powerful tools. Even though some of the topics covered here won't be used in our final version of the clip, we will still use some of our footage to learn how to apply these tools. Also, don't be concerned if the singer in the video has a slight red tinge to his skin. This is not a fault with your preview monitor as this singer does get red when he heats up a little so we shall deal with this during the chapter.

What are White Balance and Level Correction?

Just like the human eye, digital video cameras are very good at capturing color and the beautiful images that we see before us, but unlike the human eye, our camera doesn't have a highly intelligent brain attached to it. So with this in mind we have to educate our camera every time we shoot a new scene as to which color is which and at what intensity.

If you studied the Color Wheel back in primary school you may remember that if we place all of the available colors on a circular board and spin that board around its center, then the resulting board appears to be pure white. Inversely, if we shine a white light into a prism, the light will break up into the color spectrum or rainbow once it has passed through the prism. From these two observations we know that white contains all the colors of the spectrum, so it should be obvious that we need to ensure the camera knows what is white in the scene, or if nothing is white. That way the camera can deal with anything white being added to the scene. From there the camera can then accurately capture and display all the colors.

Most professional cameras have a White Balance function, where the user will hold up a white card in the scene and set the White Balance levels of the camera. However, most pro-sumer or consumer cameras have an automatic White Balance, which does a very good job at guessing what is white, but often falls short of the mark.

Even if we have used the White Balance function on your camera, sometimes a cloud may pass overhead or it becomes later in the day, which will affect the amount of light entering the camera and shining on our subject. That will in turn change the intensity of the colors we are seeing. Of course, this will slightly confuse the end result that the camera captures and will also change the intensities of the colors it is reproducing. Thankfully Vegas Pro 11 has the tools ready for you to tackle these problems.

Time for action – using the White Balance tool

Before shooting the music video clip we are editing, I did do a white balance on my camera so the colors are pretty good in the footage. But for the sake of learning the ropes we shall have a play with the White Balance plugin to see how easy it is to use:

1. If not already, open our Tutorial project and right-click on the third clip on the timeline, which is a tight shot of our singer.

2. From the drop-down menu select **Media FX**.

3. From the **List** in the **Plug-In Chooser**, double-click on **Sony White Balance** and hit the **OK** button at the top-right. We have used Media FX to ensure what we do to this clip will be applied to the entire clip from the original Take 2 track.

4. The White Balance parameters should now be open. If not, move the windows around till they are visible along with the **Preview** Window.

5. Click on the **Eye Dropper** next to the sentence **Select white color**. We need to now find something that is white in the scene. The writing on the singer's shirt under the guitar strap is white, so carefully place the lower tip of the eye dropper in the middle of one of the white letters on the shirt and click the mouse.

6. You will notice that the overall color of the scene has changed, because we have told the software which color is now white. Because I did a White Balance before shooting this footage we are really changing the colors for the worse, but it will certainly will give you an idea of how the plugin works.

7. You can now also adjust the **Amount of correction** and the **Brightness** parameters to see how they affect the scene. Once you have made some adjustments, click the checkbox on and off for the White Balance node to see the difference between the original scene and your newly-adjusted scene.

8. Once happy, you should save this preset and apply it to the long shot of the singer as those clips are from a different take. You should also apply it to the Media FX of a long shot (old take 1), insert the Sony White Balance plugin, and then select the Preset we just saved.

9. Once you have finished experimenting with the plugin, choose **Reset to None** from the preset drop list.

What just happened?

The Sony White Balance plugin is a powerful tool, especially when you are dealing with footage from consumer cameras or old video footage that you have captured into your system. You will be surprised how well it works for you and how it will bring the colors of the footage closer to how the real colors were on the day it was shot.

Have a go hero – using White Balance on your own footage or pictures

If you do have some old still photos, or even better some random video footage, import it into a new blank project and experiment with the plugin to see how it can repair your old footage's white balance.

Level correction

The whole process of capturing video with a camera, then editing it and playing it back on a TV is full of opportunities for the editor to dramatically change what the scenes look like in both good and bad ways. Probably one of the hardest parts of the whole process is making sure that what we are looking at in the preview monitor is a true representation of the colors and intensities that make up the footage, so we can correctly make adjustments to it so that our finished product looks how we expect it to when played back on someone else's TV. The better the monitor we are using, the better our chances of making the right adjustments. Having said that, we can use slightly inferior monitors as long as we know how the vision translates to other TVs.

A lesson on levels

Basically, the colors that make up the images we see on a digital TV screen are called **RGB**, which stands for **Red Green Blue**. In other words, the colors we see are a combination of these three primary colors. As we are generally using 8-bit technology for our editing and monitoring, that means that each of the three primary colors are represented by a number from 0 to 255. 0 being the lowest level equaling no color or black and the combination of the 3 values at 255 will represent white. If all three colors are set to the same value, then the output will be a variation of grey between white and black. As the values of the RGB vary from each other, we end up with a combination leading to *16,777,216* colors. For the mathematically minded that is 2,563. Each color is represented by a combination of 3 numbers. For example, black would be represented by *0, 0, 0* and white would be *255, 255, 255*. Red would be *255, 0, 0* with a value of say *196, 0, 0* representing a duller color of red.

Now that you have an understanding of how color is represented on screen, we have to consider how the software deals with this information. As is usually the case in the world of software, standards can vary from application to application. Proper levels for Computer Formats (that is web streaming, and so on) are usually represented by White = 255, 255, 255 with Black = 0, 0, 0. Sony Vegas calls this setting **Computer RGB**. For proper Digital White and Black levels in Sony Vegas, the output depends on which *CODEC* or Video Compression algorithm is being used. The Standard Sony DV Codec (which we will be using in our Tutorial project as it is the standard codec) represents white as 235, 235, 235 and black as 16, 16, 16. In other words, for the computer screen to accurately represent black and white, it adjusts the lowest level for black to 16 and the highest level for white to 235. So when we make adjustments to colors and levels, they will translate correctly to our DVD and playback on other TVs. Sony Vegas calls this setting **Studio RGB**. Let's see this in action.

Time for action – using the Levels plugin

Once again, we use the third media clip on our timeline to apply the Levels plugin:

1. Right-click on the third clip on the timeline, which is a tight shot of our singer. From the drop-down menu, select **Media FX**. The Media FX window will open for that clip, which will still contain the White Balance plugin from our previous *Time for Action* section. Make sure **White Balance** is **Unchecked**.

2. Click the **Add Plugin** button just above the small **Floppy Disk** icon and from the **Plug-In Chooser** window, double-click the **Sony Levels** plugin and hit the **OK** button at the top-right corner.

3. From the **Plug-in Preset** drop-down menu, select **Studio RGB to Computer RGB** and watch how it changes the scene in the preview monitor. Our scene now has more clarity and contrast from darks to lights. Check and uncheck the **Levels** plugin to see the difference.

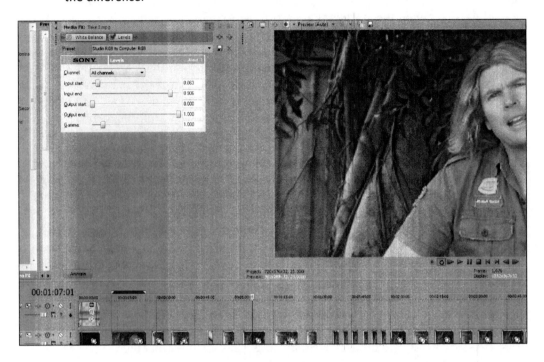

4. If you slide the **Input start** parameter to the right, you will see that the blacks become darker. If you change the **Input end** to the left the intensity increases. We shall use these parameters in our next section to ensure our level settings are correct.

5. Once again, if we were keeping these settings we would save them as a preset, apply the Levels plugin to the Media FX of our Take 1 footage (Long Shots), and apply the preset to it. This will keep all of our performance footage at the same level setting.

6. Select the **Reset to None** preset when you have finished experimenting.

What just happened?

We have compensated the Levels setting for our media to best represent the colors and contrast of our preview and ensure we are accurately adjusting our footage during the editing process. If we wanted to just apply the **Studio RGB to Computer RGB** setting to our preview monitor, another option would be to select the **Video Output FX** switch circled in the next screenshot, just to the right of the External Preview Monitor button, and apply the Levels plugin here and use the preset. This way all the footage we are seeing will have to pass through this plugin before we view it on our screen.

Remember, if you have the luxury of monitoring on a real Video Editing Monitor, then you wouldn't apply this level setting as your monitor will be representing the correct values automatically. You only need to apply the "Computer RGB" setting if you are using either your single computer monitor or the Windows Secondary Monitor as your preview window.

Another way of looking at changes to levels and colors

Besides using our eyes on the preview monitor to view the on-goings of the Levels and Colors of our video, Vegas Pro 11 offers us some technical aids in the form of **Video Scopes**. From the **View Menu** select **Video Scopes** or use *Ctrl + Alt + 2* to open the **Video Scopes** window. From the drop-down menu, select the **All** tab to reveal all four scopes. This window can be easily resized to suit your available space and to make it more readable.

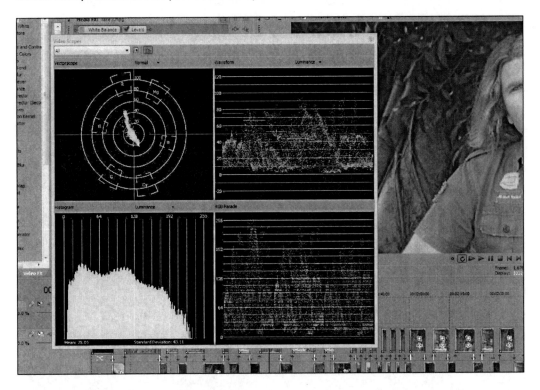

The four scopes are the **Vectorscope**, **Waveform**, **Histogram**, and the **RGB Parade**. If we are using the **Computer RGB** setting across our preview monitor, we need to select the small tab next to the drop-down menu and open the **Video Scopes Settings** window, uncheck both the **7.5 IRE setup** and the **Studio RGB** (16 to 235) boxes, and hit **OK**. This way the scopes will be accurately showing us their settings in the Computer RGB mode. The next little tab that looks like a Blue Graph, turns on or off the real time update of the scopes while the video is playing. With the **Update Scopes while Playing** tab checked, play our video from the start and watch the scopes as they show their various parameters. Once you have seen enough, place the cursor onto the third media clip on the timeline so we can look at each of the scopes and go through what they represent.

The Waveform scope

From the drop-down menu within the **Video Scopes** window, select the **Waveform** option. Now resize the window so you can see the preview monitor and the scope together.

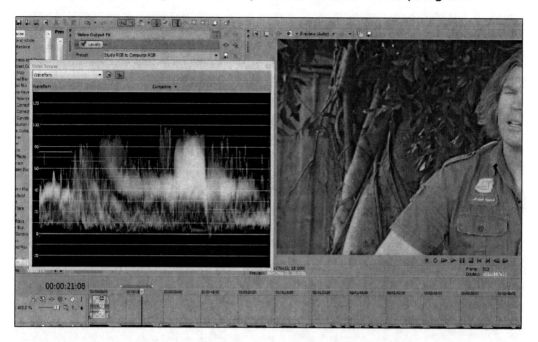

If we look closely at the Waveform scope we can see that the horizontal lines have numbers on their left-hand side. The second lowest number is 0 and the second highest number is 100. In effect these numbers represent the percentage of the levels being shown to us. 0 is representing the blacks in our video close to 0, 0, 0 and 100 represents the whites in our video close to 255, 255, 255. Let's see how our Levels plugin affects the Waveform scope.

Time for action – practical use of Levels and the Waveform scope

By applying our knowledge of colors and levels to our project, we can make accurate adjustments that suit our taste by viewing the changes in the available scopes. Let's have a closer look:

1. Right-click on the third media clip and select **Media FX**. The Media FX window will open. Move the **Scope** window so you can see the **Media FX** window, the **Video Scope** window, and your preview monitor all at once.

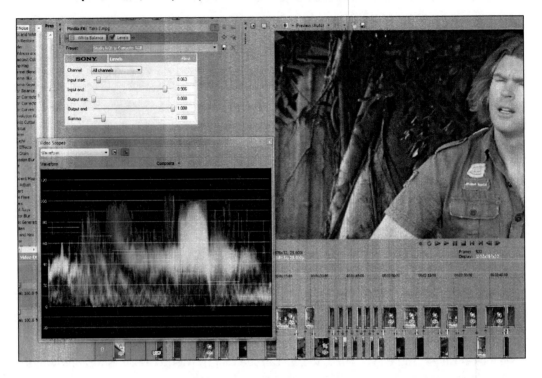

2. Make sure the **Levels** plugin is checked and select the Preset **Studio RGB to Computer RGB**. Now check and uncheck the Levels plugin and see how it changes both the Waveform and the preview monitor. Here you can see how the two things you are seeing relate to each other. With the plugin activated, the Waveform scope stretches the waveform more towards the blacks and the whites and the preview monitor contains more contrast. With the plugin unchecked, the waveform shrinks away from the extremes and the preview has less contrast and clarity.

3. With the Levels plugin checked again, slide the **Input Start** parameter to the right. You can see how the Waveform scope squashes all of the bottom of the waveform onto the 0 line and the preview gets very black in the dark areas. Inversely, by sliding the **Input end** parameter to the left, the top of the waveform squashes upwards, making the preview become very white in the light areas.

4. Once you have finished experimenting, select the **Studio RGB to Computer RGB** preset again.

What just happened?

Now that we are aware of how the Waveform scope represents what is being seen on the preview monitor, the goal is to evenly spread the waveform from top to bottom, allowing the bottom of the waveform to just touch the 0 line and some of the peaks of the waveform to just touch the 100 percent line. If you adjust the last parameter Gamma, this effectively moves the centre of the waveform up or down the percentage scale. There are no real hard and fast rules except our goal is to make the scene look as best as it can.

The RGB Parade scope

Like the Waveform scope, the RGB Parade scope is a waveform of the individual primary colors Red, Green, and Blue. So this scope allows us to see where the primary colors are sitting in relationship to each other. Use the drop-down menu in the **Video Scopes** window to select the **RGB Parade** and you will see the representation of the three primary colors. As we start to adjust and manipulate the scene with our Color Balance or Color Correction tools, we shall use this scope to see the results as shown in the next screenshot:

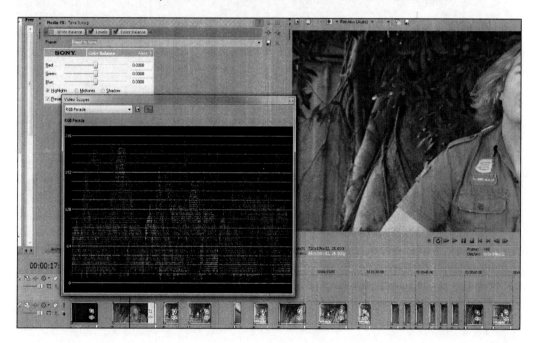

The Histogram scope

From the drop-down menu within the **Video Scopes** window, select **Histogram**. If you have ever used Photoshop or other photo editing software, you may have seen this scope before. The Histogram gives us a real time look at the amount of Luminance in the scene. The scale travels horizontally from left to right with the left-hand marker starting at 0 and the far right marker being 255, which if you recall are the numbers used to represent the levels of the RGB definitions.

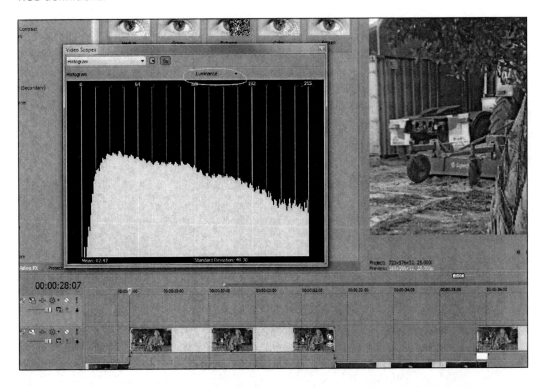

The Histogram is also very useful for adjusting the levels of a scene. You can also look at the amount of levels for each color by selecting the various color graphs from the drop menu circled in the above screenshot. For the moment we will stay on Luminance and look at how the Histogram represents what we are seeing in the preview monitor.

Time for action – using Levels and the Histogram scope on our project

As in the previous *Time for Action* section, please position the Histogram, preview monitor, and Media FX windows so that you can see them all:

1. Position the cursor so you can see the third media clip on the preview monitor. (That is the tight shot of our singer.)

2. Right-click on the third media clip and select **Media FX** from the menu.

3. If the **Levels** plugin is not inserted, do so now, and select the **Studio RGB to Computer RGB** preset.

4. Now move the cursor to the 5th media clip and do the same to it by inserting the Levels plugin to its Media FX.

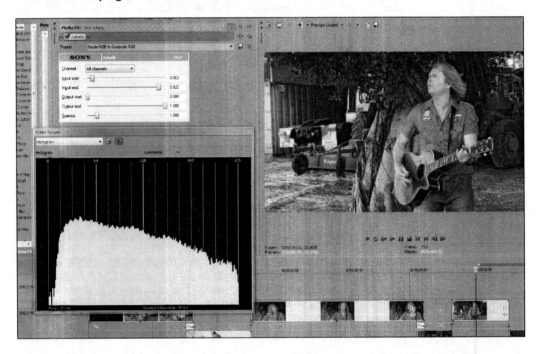

5. Now by moving the cursor between the third clip and the 5th clip, we can see the difference in their Histograms.

6. Because the tight image (third Clip) has less lighter areas in it, there is a gap between about 221 and 255 on its Histogram. On the other hand, the long shot (5th clip) has the lighter green container and the white flaps on the truck parked at the back, so its Histogram extends all the way to 255. So we understand that the more lighter areas that exist in our scene, the more the right-hand end of the Histogram fills out.

7. Now by looking at the long shot and changing the parameters of the Levels plugin, we can change its appearance to suit our tastes, but remember we don't want too much dark area or too much light area. If you over adjust these settings, then the whites and/or blacks will blow out to no detail.

8. Once you have finished experimenting, please re-select the **Studio RGB to Computer RGB** preset and save the Project.

What just happened?

We compared two scenes while looking at the preview monitor and their Histograms to see how the Histograms represent what we are seeing in the Preview window. The more we look at the scopes while we are viewing the footage, the better you will understand how they can help us adjust our parameters, making accurate changes to our edits.

Let's leave the Levels plugin inserted on our Media FX set to the Studio RGB to Computer RGB preset, as we need to keep monitoring on our computer screens accurately. Save your project here.

 Remember, if you are monitoring on a Pro Video Monitor and not typical computer monitor, you won't need the Levels plugin inserted on your media.

The Vectorscope

Of the four scopes available, the Vectorscope seems to be the most mysterious, but really it is quite a simple scope to read. It contains two values being Hue and Chroma. The first is the Hue (or color), which is represented around the circle and highlighted by the existing color positions within the green brackets, where **R** = Red. **Mg** = Magenta (red + blue), **B** = Blue, **Cy** = Cyan (blue=Green), **G** = Green, and **Yl** = Yellow (red + green). The second is the Chroma which is the intensity of the color. The duller and darker the color, and the closer to colorless, the closer the values will be to the centre and the stronger the color the further away from the centre.

Time for action – learning to read the Vectorscope

To help visually explain the use of the Vectorscope to you, let's create a Test Pattern and look at its Vectorscope. This is how we do it:

1. On the top Track of our timeline just past the end of our music video footage, right-click on the middle of the blank track and select **Insert Generated Media**.

2. From the **Plug-In Chooser**, select **Sony Test Pattern** and hit the **OK** button at the top-right of the Plug-In Chooser window.

3. From the drop-down menu within the **Video Media Generator** window, select **Color Bars PAL**.

4. Make sure that the cursor is in the middle of the new Test Pattern and look at the Vectorscope.

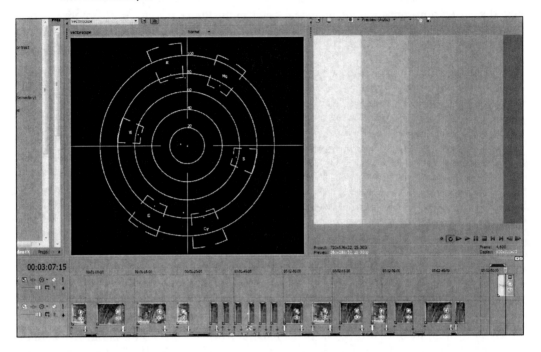

5. You will note that a white dot has appeared in every color box, plus one in the middle for the white bar. The extra few dots are representations of some of the edges where the colors meet.

6. If you now move the cursor over one of our scenes such as the third scene of the clip, you will notice that there are a lot more dots. They represent the different colors that exist within the scene with a leaning toward the red part of the Vectorscope, which is indicating the extra redness in our singer's face.

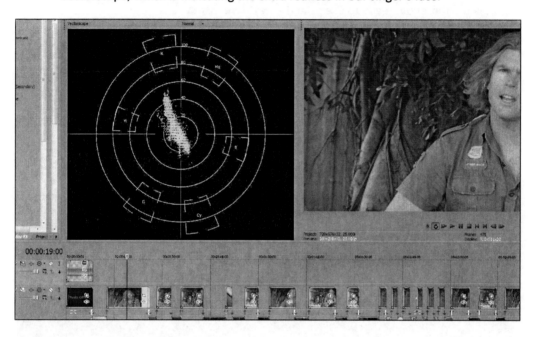

What just happened?

We inserted a Media Generator to create a Test Pattern of Line Bars onto our timeline to see how those colors were represented in the Vectorscope. By comparing what we saw here with the Vectorscope values of a scene from our project, we start to understand how the Vectorscope values are interpreting the scenes for us.

As we start to become familiar with the scopes available to us, we will learn that although each scope is a powerful tool for its purposed job, it is a combination of the scopes that will guide us to the best and most accurate adjustments. With this in mind, you will find in the drop-down menu of the Video Scopes window some useful preset combinations of the scopes laid out for you, ready to use as in the next screenshot:

Color correction and matching

Now that we have a new set of scopes to help us better understand what we are seeing, let's dive into a very important process for giving our project that professional color edge.

Color Correction and Matching was originally used to compensate for the variations in the grade and quality of the film stock used. Cheaper grades of film would saturate the colors more heavily than a better grade, and if budget cuts were introduced as a film was being shot, then the film stock suffered creating an un-acceptable variance in the colors seen on the screen. If you can find some old 1970's color movies or TV shows that were shot on film, you can often see that a blue shirt in one scene has more of a green tinge in another. The shirt hadn't changed, just the film stock and thus the variation. Also the original color correction was performed during the development and film print process. The developer would analyze each roll of film that was developed and make adjustments to the print process so the editor didn't have to worry about the color being wrong.

Today this process is done in the digital realm, even for projects still shot on film as we have more control and scope for change with these powerful tools. This can often be seen in remastered films. This process can be so precise that certain people are renowned for their Color Correction and Matching Skills and are often in demand and paid highly for their work in this area. Let's have a look at the Color Correction tool.

Time for action – color correction

By color correcting our music video clip, we can make the pictures come even more to life and add a pleasing depth to the images and quality of the end result. Let's dig into it now:

1. Let's move the cursor over the third media clip so we can see it in the preview monitor.

2. Right-click on that clip and select **Media FX**.

3. In the **Media FX** window, select the **Add FX to Plug-in Chain** button just above the **Floppy Disk** icon.

4. From the **Plug-In Chooser** select **Sony Color Correction** and hit **OK**.

5. Now we have the Color Correction tool open and you will note the three color wheels marked **Low**, **Mid**, and **High**. As their name suggests, these color wheels allow you to adjust the colors of the darker areas (Low), the mid range areas (Mid), and the lighter areas (High). Beneath each wheel you will see two eyedroppers. One with a plus sign and one with a minus sign next to it. We are going to use the Minus Eyedropper for each wheel.

6. Starting with the **High** color wheel, click on the minus eyedropper and use it to select an area on the scene which is closest to white. A good choice is the white writing on the singer's shirt. Notice that the dot in the middle of the high color wheel has moved from the centre.

7. Next do the same with the Mid minus eyedropper and select a more neutral color, close to grey, such as the piece of tree trunk just to the left of the singer's arm. Its centre dot will also move.

8. Then with the Low minus eyedropper, select something as close to black as you can find, such as some of the spaces between some of the leaves in the tree.

9. Because our footage has a pretty good color balance already, the changes this will make will be fairly subtle. However, by un-checking and re-checking the **Color Correction** plugin in the **Media FX** window, you will notice the difference. You will notice that it seems to remove an almost yellow tinge from the scene.

10. If you make sure the **Video Scopes** window, the **Media FX** window, and the preview monitor are all available to see, you can observe how switching the Color Correction plugin on and off changes the Scopes and the Scene.

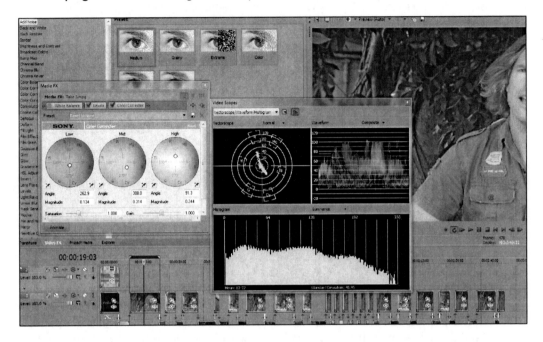

11. If you want to make some creative changes to the color of the scene, you can grab the white dots inside the color wheels and move them around the color wheel to make subtle or drastic changes.

12. With a project that has multiple scenes with different settings, the goal is to use the color correction plugin to keep the color of each scene in the whole project consistent.

What just happened?

We were able to apply the Color Correction plugin to our footage to help give the scenes a more professional color balance. At the same time we learned to look at our scopes to see how these subtle changes are represented numerically.

Have a go hero – fine tuning using the color correction tool

Once you are happy with your color correction of the scene, save the preset and then apply it to the Media FX track of the long shots of the singer so that that both angles of the performance look the same. If the long shot looks too different from the tight shot after applying the saved preset, use the color wheels to make some subtle adjustments till you are happy.

Color Corrector Secondary plugin: Reducing the red

Now that we have a good look happening for our clip, we need to address the red texture our singer's skin has to it. There are a few ways to approach this, but the best way is to apply the **Color Corrector Secondary** plugin to the footage to isolate and adjust the skin tone.

Time for action – removing the redness using the Color Corrector Secondary plugin

1. As we have done in the past, right-click on the third clip on the timeline and select Media FX.

2. Add the **Color Corrector Secondary** plugin to the FX chain.

3. Just below the color wheel, use the **Eyedropper** tool next to **Select Effect Range**, and sample a spot of the singer's red skin on his cheek.

4. Check the box below the Eyedropper called **Show Mask**. The scene will become black with a hint of the outline of the skin showing.

5. In the **Limit Luminance** section set the **Low** parameter to **118.6**, **High** parameter to **255.0**, and **Smooth** parameter to **15.1**.

6. In the **Limit Hue** section, set **Center** to **111.7**, **Width** to **10.0**, and **Smooth** to **10.0**. You will now start to see the inverse image of the singer's skin. See the next screenshot:

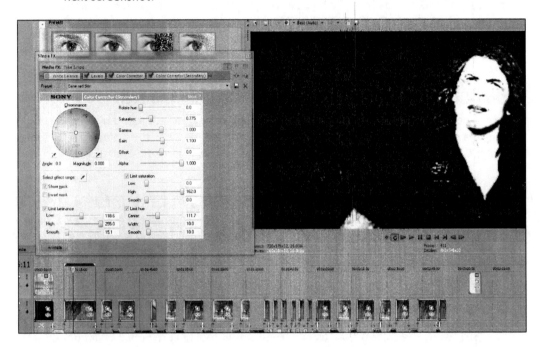

7. Uncheck the **Show Mask** box. Nothing will have changed yet except we can now see our scene normally again.

8. Adjust the **Saturation** parameter to **0.775** and watch the skin of the singer become paler and less red. If you hold the *Ctrl* key as you slide the parameter, it will move in small increments. If you play the video, you will see that this now tracks the skin tone and adjusts it for the whole video for this take.

9. If you are happy with the skin color, save this preset and apply it to the long shot of the singer. And save your project. If it isn't too your taste, make some subtle adjustments to the **Saturation** or the **Limit Hue Center** parameters.

10. This plugin can also be used in a creative way for re-coloring any item within the scene. If you grab the dot in the middle of the color wheel and slide it towards the blue section, you will see that the singers skin now takes on a blue Smurf-like color, or any color you select from the wheel. Reselect the just saved parameter before moving on.

What just happened?

Using the Color Corrector Secondary plugin, we were able to isolate the skin texture of the subject and adjust just that part of the scene to remove the redness from his skin tone. We then applied it to the other long shot take to make our project color.

Summary

We learned a lot in this chapter about how to address the color of our footage in both a corrective and creative manner.

Specifically, we covered White Balance and Levels, their importance to the video's final output, and how to ensure they are sitting at acceptable levels. We examined the Video Scopes available to you in Vegas Pro 11 and how to read them in conjunction with our adjustments. The Color Correction tool with both its simplicity of use, but also its wide range of parameters was an important section. We also looked at the Color Corrector Secondary tool and how this powerful plugin can be used for corrective and creative adjustments with its ability to select specific color ranges to adjust within our footage.

Now that we have brought our project closer to being the pro-looking music video clip that it should be, we can move forward to learn a few more tricks and creative choices we can make for the video before we tackle the powerful Audio tools available to us in Vegas Pro 11.

7

Look, I Made it Move!!—Automating Tools in Sony Vegas

In days gone by, the only way to make your film move in any way was to do it at the time of shooting. Panning the camera from left, right or moving it up and down, or zooming in or out had to be performed by the camera man. Now, because of digital editing we have the tools that allow us to create all these movements and many more during the editing process.

In this chapter, we shall look at the many ways to animate or move all sorts of things within Sony Vegas Pro 11, such as:

- Pan/crop and zooming automation
- Parameter automation
- Applying an effect and animating it
- Track Motion, Make Compositing Child settings
- Motion blur

So let's get moving...

Pan/crop and zooming automation

Some of the shots in our music video project are a little long without any camera movement. So we need to create some movement, which will take away that lingering waiting for something to happen feeling you often get when a scene remains static for too long.

Let's point out those longish shots and learn the pan/crop Automation process.

Time for action – automating the pan/crop tool

With our tutorial project open, zoom out the whole project so that all of the events can be seen on the timeline. You will notice that some of the events are longer than others. Our third event is actually one of the longest media clips in the project so let's look at this event first.

Zooming

Although the action of zooming is usually left to the camera operator, we can also create powerful camera moves in the editing stage. Here we will show you how:

1. As we have mentioned and seen in previous chapters, each media clip has two icons on its right-hand side. The lower one is **Event FX** and the upper one is the one we want, **Event Pan/Crop**. Click on this icon.

2. The **Event Pan/Crop** window will open, which we have seen before in our earlier chapters. This window contains the scene with a large **F** over the frame, and the bounding box has eight little square handles around it available for adjustment. Along the bottom of the window you will notice a time line with the word **Position** on the far left. The timeline cursor also has a tab at the top.

3. Grab the timeline cursor tab and slide it to the left. You will notice that the video updates itself as you move the cursor. Slide the cursor all the way to the right. See the yellow circled tab in the following screenshot:

4. What this cursor does is tells the system that you are about to put a keyframe in that position. A **keyframe** is a piece of data that the system uses to set up the position of our **Event Pan/Crop** parameters, or any automation data we chose to change throughout the whole system. At the beginning of the timeline you will see that there is a small diamond on the position track circled as black in the previous screenshot. This is the keyframe that tells the program what position the **Event Pan/Crop** parameters are set to for this media clip. Every media clip will have a keyframe at its beginning.

5. With our cursor still at the end of the timeline in the **Event Pan/Crop** window, grab the top-right handle of the frame and drag it towards the centre of the scene by about a third.

6. Click and hold anywhere inside the now smaller frame. A new cursor with arrows pointing left, right, up, and down will appear. Slide it to center the frame closer to the singers face, making sure that the edges of the frame don't go outside the scene. See the following screenshot:

7. You will also see that a new keyframe diamond has appeared beneath the **Cursor** tab. Grab the **Cursor** tab and slowly slide it to the left and watch the **Preview Monitor**. The scene will now zoom out.

8. If you now play the video from just before our third clip, you will see that we have created a smooth camera zoom starting in the normal position for the scene and finishing closer and centred on the singers face. The zoom continues for the duration of the media clip.

9. We can now change the duration of the zoom by simply moving the last keyframe diamond to the left. With your mouse, click and hold the last keyframe and move it to the left to about the **00:00:08:00** mark on the **Event Pan/Crop** window timeline.

10. Now play and watch the video. The zoom will happen a bit faster, then once it reaches the second keyframe, it will stay at that zoom.

11. The keyframes are also editable entities; in that they can be copied, pasted, and deleted Let's click on the first keyframe at **00:00:00:00** to copy and paste it at **00:00:12:00** and to create a zoom in and then out effect. Left-mouse click on the diamond keyframe at the beginning of the **Position** timeline track of the **Event Pan/Crop** window to make it active. Now right-mouse click and select **Copy**.

12. Left-mouse click on the position track close to the **00:00:12:00** mark then right-click there and paste the keyframe. The cursor will jump here as well.

13. Once again play the clip and watch what the zoom does in the preview monitor. Let's remove the last keyframe as it makes it feel unnatural, and move the keyframe at **00:00:08:00** back to the end at **00:00:12:00**. To delete the keyframe, right-click on it and select **Delete** from the drop-down menu.

14. Another thing we can do is to swap the first and last keyframe around to change the zoom in to a zoom out. Drag the first keyframe and move it all the way to the end, then drag the second keyframe and drag it all the way to the beginning and play the clip.

15. Let's swap the keyframes back again to keep the zoom in. If you use the *Ctrl + Z* keys it will undo the slides you did and return the keyframes. Click on *Ctrl + Z* the same number of times as you made moves to bring it back to the way it was. Another useful function is that we can copy these keyframes to another media clip.

16. Select the first keyframe diamond, then while holding the *Shift* key, select the second. A white dot will appear inside both diamonds.

17. Right-click one of the keyframes and select copy. We now have these two keyframe settings in a clipboard.

18. Select the **Pan/Crop** icon of the 8th media clip that starts at **00:00:40:00**.

19. In the **Event Pan/Crop** window right-click onto the keyframe at **00:00:00:00** and select **Paste**. We have now applied the zoom in from media clip 3 to this new clip. Play the video from just before the new clip and watch the result.

20. Even though this clip is shorter in length than the third clip, the paste function used in the previous step moves the right-hand keyframe to land right at the end of the media clip timeline. You can apply this paste function to any media clip that you would like to have the same zoom applied to it.

Panning left to right

The action of panning the camera from left to right or even up and down can be added in post production. Let's have a look at this tool and how we can make a static image look even slicker:

1. In the same way that we zoomed with the **Event Pan/Crop** window we can create a camera pan either from side-to-side or top-to-bottom.

2. Let's create a pan on the long shot clip that starts at **00:00:35:19** by clicking on its **Event Pan/Crop** icon.

3. Left-mouse click onto the keyframe at the very beginning of the **Event Pan Crop** timeline to make it active.

4. Now if we started to pan the frame in its current size, then the pan would move off the scene and start to show a black background, which isn't what we want. With this in mind we need to crop the starting frame to be smaller so that it leaves room for the pan to happen. So grab the top-left handle of the frame, size the frame to about 75 percent its original size, and slide it to the left as a starting point. See the following screenshot:

5. As in the zoom, move the timeline **Cursor** tab of the **Event Pan/Crop** window all the way to the right-hand side.

6. Slide our smaller frame so it is just touching the right-hand edge of the scene.

7. Play the video and watch the camera pan from left-to-right.

8. Obviously a combination of the pan and zoom would be very easy to do by making the end keyframe position even smaller thus making the scene both pan left-to-right and zoom in slightly.

9. We can use this same method to slide graphics, text, or any image we desire to move around the screen. By having a static or even slightly moving colored background on a lower track, we can place some text or a still photo on a higher track and move the higher track image around the screen. We often see this technique used in TV commercials or even 2D animations.

10. One more parameter on the keyframe will also help to make our zoom and/or pan more camera like. By right-clicking on the end keyframe of our last pan, we will see a set of values in the drop-down menu starting with **Linear**, **Fast**, **Slow**, **Smooth**, **Sharp**, and **Hold**. By selecting one of these setting, the keyframe will change slightly how it responds. Let's select **Smooth** and play back the clip again. You will notice that the zoom is no longer **Linear** and travelling at the exact same speed from start-to-finish. Instead it starts a little bit slower, speeds up ever so slightly, and then starts to slow down as it reaches the end of the pan. In effect doing what a camera operator would do naturally! Go ahead and try each of the selections and see how they affect the pan on our clip. Set it back to **Smooth** when you have finished experimenting and save the project.

What just happened?

We used the **Event Pan/Crop** tool, which is available for every media clip on the timeline . With this tool we learned to create digital zooms and pans using keyframes. This method of creating keyframes is an important one to master as it is used in all tools and plugin FX of Vegas Pro 11 that have parameters that can be automated/animated.

Have a go hero – doing more with video panning

Now is the time to go through all of our media clips, especially the longer shots, and add a pan or zoom to their **Event Pan/Crop**. Remember not to zoom in too close as it will result in a slightly blurry result due to the pixel resolution on the screen, which we discussed back in Chapter 2, *Let the Magic Begin: Beginning the Project and Acquiring Media*. Also be aware of the scenes that already have a real camera zoom in them as adding a digital zoom on top of that can be too much and make the scene very un-natural.

Parameter automation

In the same way that we have just automated or animated some movement in our **Event Pan/Crop** window, we can animate most parameters within an FX plugin. Here we are going to add an FX to the whole track and automate the parameters to turn on and off that FX at certain locations in the Video Timeline. This Parameter Animation can be applied to both the Video Track FX and the Video Event FX windows.

Time for action – automating parameters

Let's add an old film effect to our studio scenes to give them an even more different feel. For the purpose of this exercise, let's add the plug-in to the whole track and we will use the parameter automation to turn the effect on and off when the appropriate scenes happen:

1. Click on the track 3 **Track FX** button and from the plug-in chooser double-click on the **Sony Film Effects** plug-in, and then hit the **OK** button.

2. Position your cursor over the second media clip (which is the guitarist in studio close up) so you can see it in the **Preview Monitor**.

3. In the **Video Track FX** window select **Circa 1980** from the **Preset** drop-down menu. You can also make adjustments to the parameters, such as the amount of dust particles, grain, and the tint.

4. The scene will take on a bluish tinge that is a hallmark of film from around 1980. The only problem is that every media clip on the track 3 timeline now has the plugin applied.

5. At the bottom of the **Video FX Track** window click on the **Animate** button.

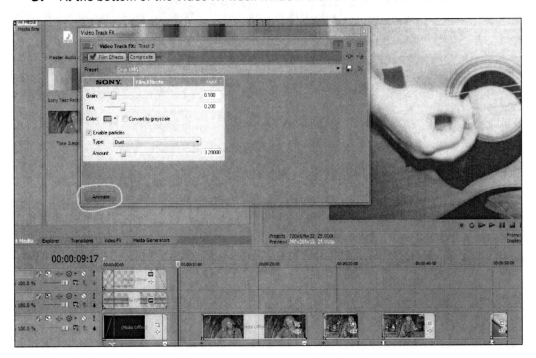

6. A film effects timeline will appear at the bottom of the **Video Track FX** window.

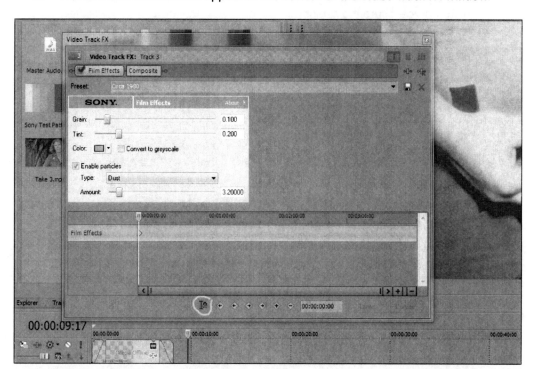

7. Please note that there is a keyframe node at the beginning of the timeline, which has set the **Circa 1980** preset from the beginning. The first frame on the main timeline is a scene of the singer performing, which we don't want to have the film effects on. Let's change the preset to **Reset to None**. This will keep the film effects set to no effect at the beginning of the video so that we can now use a new keyframe to turn the **Circa 1980** preset on when needed further along the timeline.

This next piece of information is very important so please read very carefully to avoid issues when using the animation of any parameters.

8. In the previous screenshot I have circled a button in yellow at the bottom of the **Video Track FX** window, which is the **Sync Cursor** button. It will lock the timing of the automation cursor in the Video Track FX window with the main timeline cursor. It makes sure that the timeline cursor in the **Video Track FX** window moves to the exact same time position as the main editing time line cursor. If you click on the **Sync Cursor** button now, the cursor will jump forward on the film effects timeline to correspond with the cursor position of the main timeline cursor.

9. The main thing you need to do is not change any parameters of the plug-in until you are 100 percent sure the cursor is in the right position, otherwise it will place a new keyframe in positions you don't want and it can get confusing as to which one's you want to have and which you don't.

10. Place the cursor on the main timeline about halfway through the transition between the first and second media clip.

11. In the **Film Effects** window select **Circa 1980** from the **Preset** window.

12. You will notice that the **Circa 1980** look is now applied to our video and a new keyframe diamond appears on the **Film Effects** timeline. But we aren't there yet.

13. Play the video from the beginning and you will see that the **Film Effects** plug-in gradually turns on as it gets closer to the second media clip. This is not what we want.

14. Right-click on the first keyframe diamond and from the drop-down menu choose **Hold**. Do the same for the next keyframe diamond as well. The keyframes will turn red, as in the next image, to let you know that they have a setting applied to them. Play the video from the beginning and watch how the effect now turns on at the appropriate position.

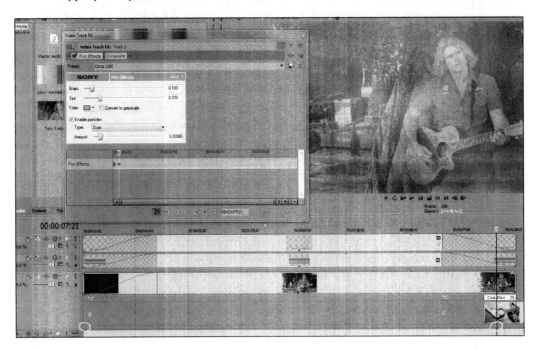

15. You will also see that a couple of small keyframe diamonds have been placed on the main timeline at the bottom of that track. See the yellow circles in the previous screenshot.

16. Now place the main cursor at the very end on the second media clip and from the Film Effect's **Preset** select **Reset to None** again. The new keyframe will also be red as it is smart enough to realize the previous keyframe was set to **Hold**.

17. Now play the video from the beginning and you will see that our **Film Effects** will turn on and off at the beginning and end of the second media clip.

18. This method of applying keyframes and setting each keyframe with a different parameter setting applies to every plugin parameter available in the Vegas Pro 11 on both video and audio media clips.

What just happened?

We have just seen how to apply effect parameter automation to the **FX** window. This same process applies to both the **Track FX** and the **Event FX** windows. You can also have multiple plugins on each track or event and each FX will have its own keyframe track on the animate timeline in the **FX** window.

Now that we are adding more **FX** to our project and depending on the processing power of the computer, you may experience some timing issues with the lip sync and or the smoothness of the video playback in your **Preview Monitor**. This is quite normal, especially if your CPU isn't very powerful. The best solution is to use the most powerful computer you can access and lower the quality of the **Preview Monitor** to help compensate for the lack of power. Watching your preview in the **Draft** mode can be annoying, but at least you can see what your movements are doing.

Have a go hero – doing more with FX automation (animation)

Now you can go through each of the recording studio scenes and apply the **Film Effects** plugin, remembering to turn it on and off at the exact beginning and end positions. Remember to save the project as you successfully set up each clip, so that you can revert back to the same position if you make a mistake. Also once you have finished, turn off the cursor lock in the **Video Track FX** window to make sure no keyframes are accidentally added next time you open up this window. Also remember to save your project once you have finished applying the automation to the **Film Effects** plugin for the whole project.

The Track Motion Tool

Another tool available to us is the **Track Motion** tool. Rather than moving individual elements we can move the whole media clip around the viewing area in many different ways.

Time for action – using Track Motion to move two tracks together

The **Track Motion** tool is similar to the **Pan/Crop** tool except it is ideal for moving a grouped set of clips on different tracks together. Let's apply that technique now:

1. Click the **Track Motion** icon of our second track (see yellow circle in the following screenshot):

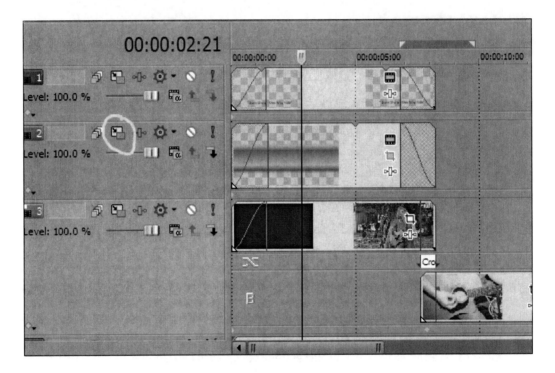

2. The **Track Motion** window will open. You will recall that we used this window in the previous chapter to add the drop shadow to the orange text bar. This window offers us a variety of parameters that allow us to change the orientation and position of the media on that track.

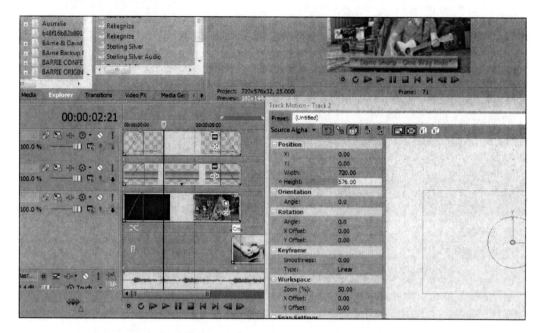

3. The **Track Motion** window is divided into six separate sections including **Position**, **Orientation**, **Rotation**, **Keyframe**, **Workspace**, and **Snap Settings**.

4. The **Position**, **Rotation**, and **Workspace** are identical to the same parameters in the **Pan/Crop** tool. If you manipulate the numbers while being able to see the **Preview Monitor** you can see how each parameter affects the orange text bar. The **X** and **Y** parameters under **Position** will move the media left-and-right or up-and-down. **Rotation** and **Orientation** will change position in a circular motion. You will notice that the orange bar is moving but the actual text stays stationary. This is because the text is on the first track and doesn't see our movements.

5. Now click on the **Make Compositing Child** icon on track two and circled in yellow in the following screenhot:

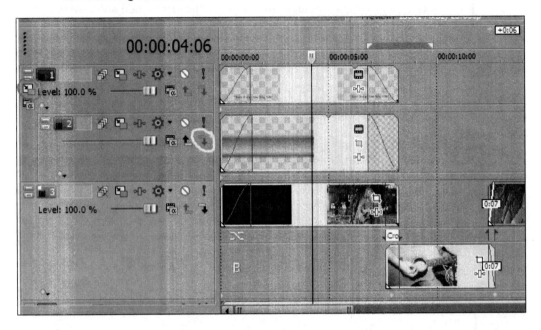

6. You will notice that the header of track two is now indented and the arrow pointing upwards next to the icon we just pushed is now highlighted. Also a new **Track Motion** icon has appeared circled in red that is called **Parent Motion**. In effect, we have made track two a child of track one. That means anything we do to the **Parent Motion** parameters will change both tracks at the same time. So let's slide the orange bar and text in and out of the scene using the **Parent Motion** parameters.

7. Click on the red circled **Parent Motion** icon. The **Parent Track Motion** window will open, which looks identical to the standard **Track Motion** window and containing the same set of parameters.

8. Change the **X** parameter of the **Position** section by either typing the number into the parameter box or by clicking on the drop arrow beside the **X** parameter. Use the slide tool that appears to slide the orange text bar off to the left of the preview monitor so it can't be seen in the monitor. A value of around **-1020** should do it.

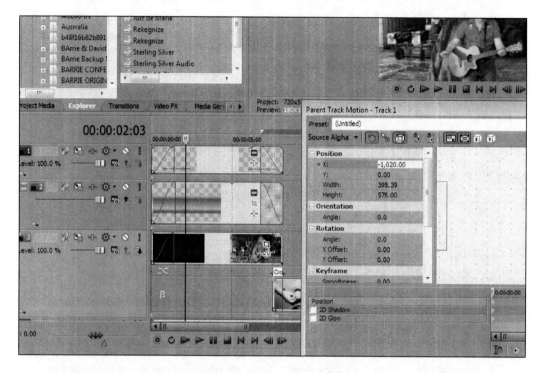

9. Now using the animation process we have used already in our project, let's turn on the sync cursor and place our main cursor on the timeline about a quarter of the way along the orange bar media clip of track two at around **00:00:01:21**.

10. Change the **X** parameter back to read **0.00** and you will see that the orange text bar reappears on the **Preview Monitor**.

11. Copy the keyframe diamond at **00:00:01:21** and paste it at **00:00:05:21** on the animation timeline of the **Parent Track Motion** Window. See the yellow circle in the following screenshot:

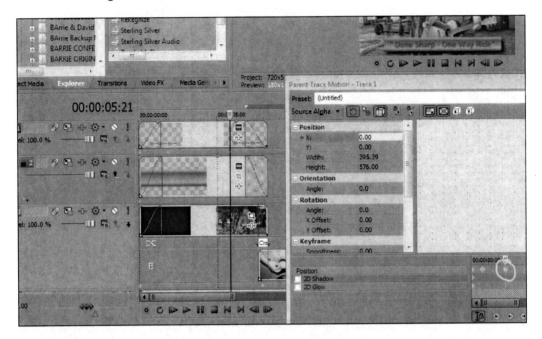

12. Add one more keyframe at **00:00:08:05** and change the **X** parameter to **+1,020.00**.

13. Turn off the sync cursor in the **Parent Track Motion** window and play the project from the beginning. You will now see the orange text bar with the text slide in and slide out at our newly added keyframe points.

14. Without the **Make Compositing Child** function and the **Parent Track Motion** tools, we would have to apply the same parameter changes to each track individually. That can be tedious, especially if we had three or four tracks representing an object on the screen.

15. The other beauty is that we can now add tracks to the parent track and they will respond to the changes automatically.

16. To show you what I mean, click on the **Make Compositing Child** icon on track three and play the project from the start again. You will see that all the media will slide in and out.

17. Once you have done this, turn off the **Make Compositing Child** icon again for track three and save the project.

What just happened?

We have just looked at the **Track Motion** parameters and used them to create an animation of our lower third text block which is made up of media resting on two different tracks. The Make Compositing Child function allowed us to apply the motion settings to one Parent Track Motion window which in turn applied those movements to both tracks simultaneously! As you use these parameters more, your imagination will discover new ways to apply these settings to your project. Remember, the animation of media such as text and overlays can really add a professional edge to your project, so gaining a good understanding of applying these techniques will serve you well in your quest to be a great editor.

The Motion Blur Tool

As with anything moving in the real world, if an object flies past you very quickly, even the naked eye will see a blurred effect on that object. So to have anything moving quickly in the video, adding a Blur to the motion will greatly enhance its natural feel and look. Sony Vegas Pro 11 caters for this by supplying a Motion Blur tool. For example, if you use track motion or event pan/crop to move a clip across the frame, each frame is displayed clearly when no motion blur is applied. Turning on motion blur adds a motion-dependent blur to each frame to create the appearance of smooth motion in the same way a fast-moving subject is blurred when you take a photograph with a slow shutter speed.

Time for action – adding Motion Blur

A little different to other effects we have discussed so far, Motion Blur is applied not to the individual clips but to the whole project, and it appears on the Video Bus Track:

1. Use Ctrl + Shift + B and the Video Bus Track will appear under the last video track on the time line.

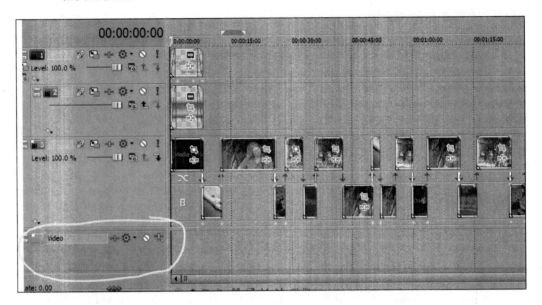

2. Right mouse click in the middle of this track and select "**Insert / Remove Envelope**" and from the drop down menu choose **Motion Blur Amount**.

3. At the bottom of the Video Bus Track you will now see a pink Line which is the envelope to control the amount of Motion Blur that will be applied to your project.

4. You can click on this line and move it upwards to around the **00:00:00:06** mark

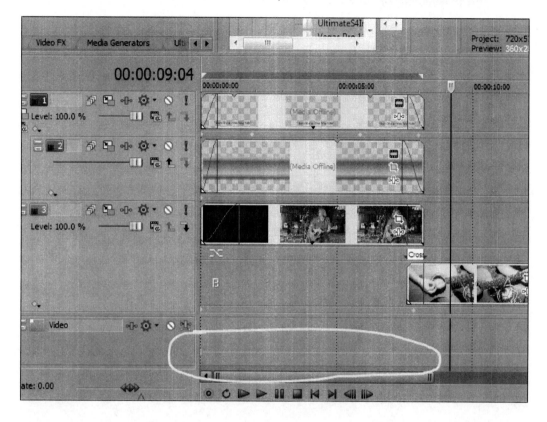

5. You can add edit points to make the envelope increase or decrease at various points on the line. For example, we only want the blur to be applied to the orange box and text sliding into and out of the picture. We can add edit points by double clicking on the pink line to raise or lower the envelope.

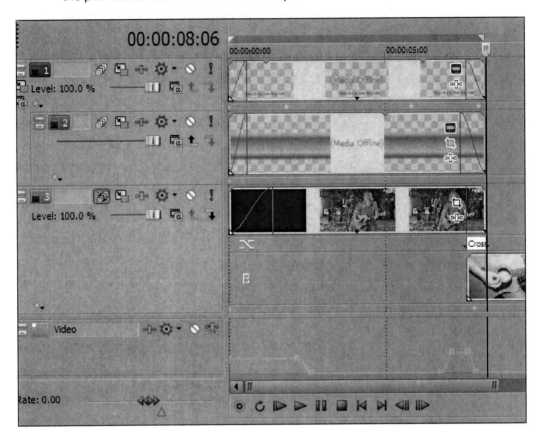

6. Remember this applies the blur effect to every track that goes through the Video Bus. If you don't want the blur to be applied to a particular track, each track has a bypass motion blur switch on its header, highlighted in the next picture in red. By turning this bypass on, that track won't have the Blur applied to it.

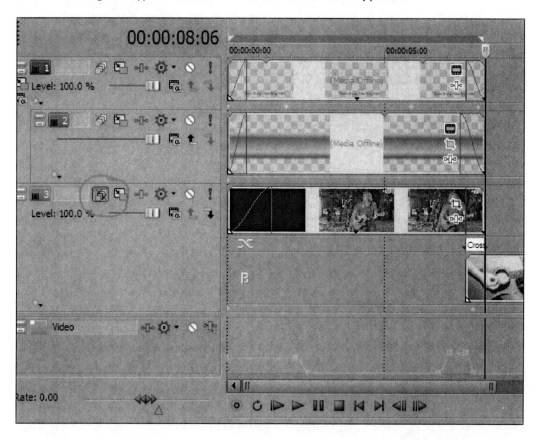

7. Applying the Motion Blur to animated objects really brings that animation into the realm of reality, but it can also be applied to footage. For example, if the scene was shot from the passenger seat of a fast moving car, you can emphasize the speed of the car by applying Motion Blur which will blur street signs and any objects passing by the windows of the car.

8. Also the kind of Blur can be changed to suit the footage. If you go to the **Project Properties** (Alt + Enter) you will see a drop down menu next to Motion Blur Type.

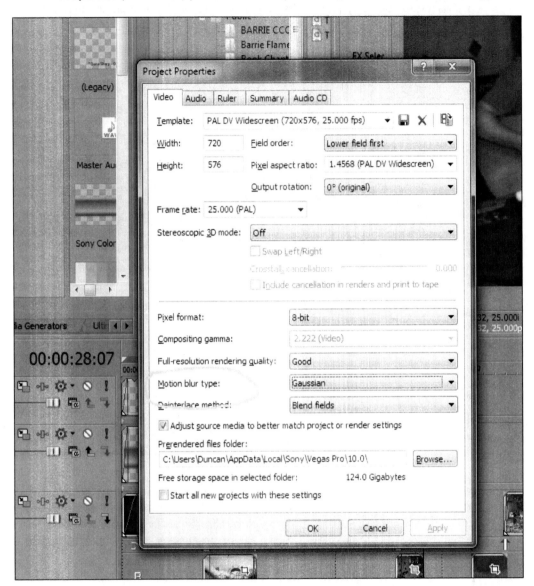

9. This drop-down list contains three blur types: Gaussian, Pyramid, and Box and the same three with the Asymmetric extension. Gaussian is the most used blur, but feel free to experiment with the other types to see how they apply to your animations or footage.

What just happened?

We just learned how to apply the Motion Blur effect to our project, which is a fantastic feature to help enhance our animations and or moving footage.

Summary

We learned a lot in this chapter about using Automation to Move and Animate the tools in Vegas Pro 11.

Specifically, we covered:

- Pan / Crop and Zooming Automation to give your project that pro look
- Parameter Automation, which allows for small or large effect changes real time
- Applying an effect and animating it. Bringing the most from the motion Tools of effects
- Track Motion, Make Compositing Child settings. Unleashing the hidden potential of Track Motion Tools
- Adding reality to the movement of objects with Motion Blur

Once you are feeling confident with the principals we have covered in this chapter, let's move on to the world of audio in the next chapter.

8

The Importance of Audio

Even during the days of silent movies, the producers realized the importance of music and sound. So much so that while the silent movie was being shown at the theatre, musicians and actors would "Live at the Theatre", creating the sound FX and music to give the viewer a full cinema experience. Vegas Pro 11 certainly has a full arsenal of audio tools at your disposal. In this chapter we shall delve into the pros and cons of audio for vision and take a first look at these powerful tools.

In this chapter we shall work with:

- Concepts of audio
- Audio 101
- The **EQ** plugin
- The **Compression** and **Gate** plugin
- The mixing console
- Insert **FX**
- **Input Bus** and recording
- I/O
- Automation, read/write (Touch and Latch)
- Mute and solo
- Volume and pan
- Creating a final mix

So let's get on with it...

Concepts of audio

The power of audio in film and television certainly becomes very apparent when you turn the volume down. A movie without its soundtrack, FX track, dialogue track, and ambient tracks, starts to create a void in the experience. Especially nowadays with nearly everyone having a surround sound theatre system in their lounge, or media room!

So to ensure that you can make the most form the audio tools in Vegas Pro 11, I will first give you a 101 of the basics and physics of audio. A good understanding of this basic knowledge will hold you in good stead and you will no longer be just guessing when you change the parameters of the audio plugins.

As the audio of our beginners guide video clip is already finalized, please download the audio tutorial bundle files to use once we start the *Time for Action* section of this chapter.

Audio 101

Just like the waves created in water when a stone is dropped into it, sound travels through the air in a similar way, but also in a three dimensional manner. Starting at a sound source, such as the words coming from a speaker through to the sound of a full orchestra, without air particles around us the sound wouldn't be able to travel from the source to our ear.

Just like the waves on the water, sound is often represented as a sine wave travelling through the air, and that sine wave represents the volume and duration of the sound over time.

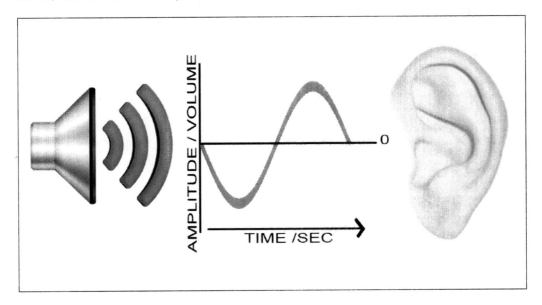

The red sine wave in the middle of the previous screenshot represents one cycle, which is also known as 1 Hertz (Hz). That is the time it takes the sound to start at zero, travel to its lowest volume, then back up through zero to its maximum volume, and then back to zero. So the previous screenshot represents 1 Hz or 1 cycle per second. Sound that can be heard by the human ear falls within the range of 20Hz up to 20,000 Hz. The upper frequencies are referred to as 20 kilo Hertz or 20 kHz.

Time for action – load and listen to the tones file

To help you understand this principal, let's start a new project to deal with the Audio functions:

1. Make sure you have downloaded the audio tutorial bundle from the Packt Publishing website. Unzip the files to a place on your system that you can access from within Vegas Pro 11.

2. Start Vegas Pro 11 and on the keyboard select *Ctrl + N* to start a new session.

3. The **New Project** window will open. Here you can set the video to whatever you like, but for this Tutorial make sure the **Audio** tab is set to **48000** as **Sample Rate(Hz)** and **16** as **Bit depth**. Hit the **OK** button.

4. Now save the project and call it **Audio Tutorial**. You can save it in the same folder as where the audio tutorial files live.

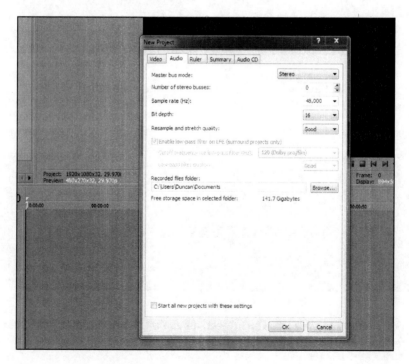

5. Now click on the **Explorer** tab and point the explorer to where you have unzipped the audio tutorial files.

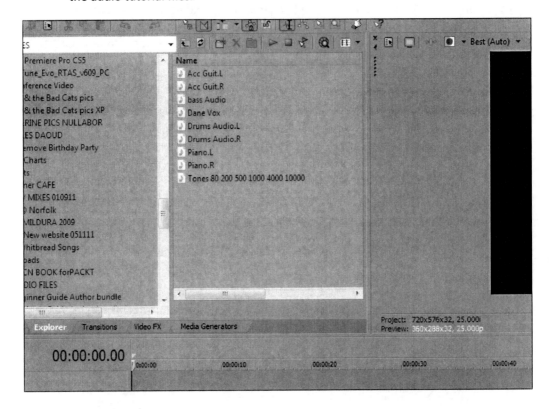

6. From the list of files click-and-drag to the timeline a file called **Tones 80 200 500 1000 4000 10000**.

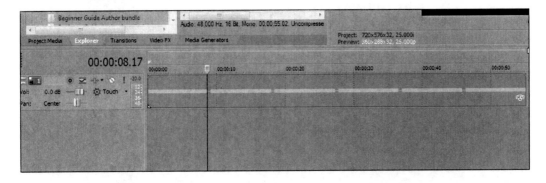

7. Upon bringing the file into the project, an audio track is automatically created for the **Tones 80 200 500 1000 4000 10000** file to rest upon.

8. Ensure your speakers aren't too loud and play this file from the beginning. You will hear a sequence of six sine wave tones including 80Hz, 200Hz, 500Hz, 1,000Hz, 4,000Hz, and 10,000Hz. Each tone will run for around eight seconds with a small gap before the next tone will begin. As each tone is playing, imagine the sine waves flying from the speakers or headphones into your ears. That is 80 sine waves per second followed by 200 waves per second, 500 waves per second, and so on until the ear piercing 10,000 waves per second. As the frequency increases so does the pitch. So the higher the frequency of the waves passing your ears the higher the pitch. Of course I have only selected six tones from the 19,980 separate frequencies that the ear can hear starting at 20Hz and finishing at 20,000 Hz (20 kHz).

What just happened?

Here we just refreshed our memory on how to import media files into a project by bringing an audio media clip onto the timeline. By playing this file we now begin to have an understanding of how individual frequencies sound and their relationship to each other, which will lead us to our next topic, equalization.

Equalization

Equalization (aka EQ) as discussed in the previous section, shows us that sound is often represented in sine waves. Although a flute or a low bass drone may be close to a sine wave, most sounds are a complex mixture of a variety of frequencies. If for example, we were to play all six of our tones at the same time, our standard sine wave would turn into something more complex.

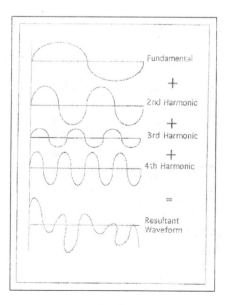

Although sine waves are a good way to represent sound, in reality the waves of the human voice, ambient noise, or pretty much any complex sound has a wave that isn't as simple as a sine wave.

The art of Equalisation or EQ, began its life as a tool for repairing sound or as the name suggests, bringing the sound back into a state of equilibrium; whereas today it has become more of a creative tool, for carving out a sound from a recording. Usually our first encounter with EQ is on a home stereo or portable audio device where we have the ability to boost or reduce the bass and/or the treble of our music. There are often preset EQ settings named after the style of music that EQ would suit such as, jazz, rock, pop, dance, and so on. EQ is best described as a volume for particular frequencies. Just as we turn the volume of our overall music up or down, the EQ has a volume that is centred at a particular frequency. The bass parameter on an iPod for example, is usually centred at 100Hz whereas the treble is usually centred at 10 kHz. To accurately adjust the frequencies that we would like, we need a tool that allows us to change the volume of a particular frequency. This is where the **EQ plugin** comes in.

Every audio track when it is created in Vegas Pro 11 by default comes with three plugins already inserted into the **Track** FX. They are **Track Noise Gate**, **Track EQ**, and **Track Compressor**. These three plugins are used on pretty much every audio track, so they are pre inserted to save your time. Let's look at the audio track and its plugins.

Time for action – using the EQ plugin to equalize a guitar sound

The best way to get to know how EQ effects audio is to apply it to specific sounds. Here we shall do just that with the sounds in our project:

1. Make sure our new audio tutorial project is open. If the **Tones** clip is still on the timeline then delete it from the timeline and let's use the **Explorer** tab to drag the **Acc Guit** clip from our audio tutorial files onto the timeline.

2. Once on the time line, slide the media clip all the way to the left so it is hard against the track header. Double-click onto the **Acc Guit** media clip, which represents the acoustic guitar track and select the **loop** function below the timeline, circled in yellow in the following screenshot:

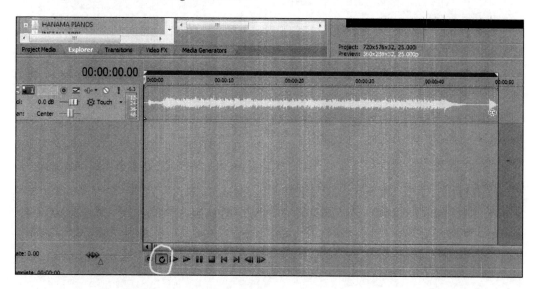

3. This **loop** function is very handy when replaying a section of a project over and over so we don't have to keep restarting the playback. In this example, as soon as the cursor reaches the end of the **Acc Guit** clip it will jump back to the start of the clip and keep playing from there.

4. Now just like our video tracks, there are a couple of ways to apply effects to this clip. We can either add it in the **Track FX Insert** or on the **Event FX Insert**. Here we will use the **Track FX**.

5. Click on the **Track FX** icon on the track header and our **Audio Track FX** box will open to reveal the pre-inserted plugins discussed previously. Select the **Track EQ** tab:

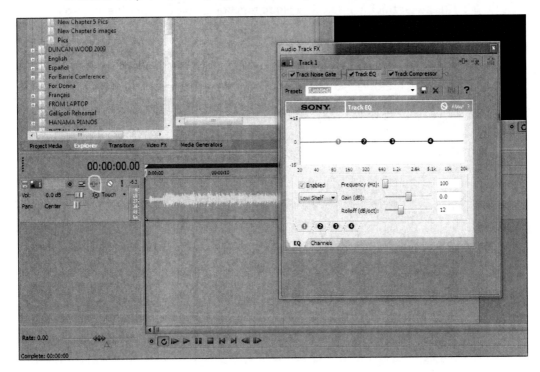

6. You will notice that the **Track EQ** has four dots representing the four EQ bands that can be adjusted. The red dot is the currently active band that changing parameters will affect. You will also notice the four tabs that represent each band and allow you to select the four different EQ bands. You can select which EQ band by clicking on the dots on the EQ line.

7. Parameters can be changed by moving the three sliders under the EQ graphic, or an even easier method is to click and hold the numbered dot and move it around. Let's click the number **4** dot and slide it up and a little to the left.

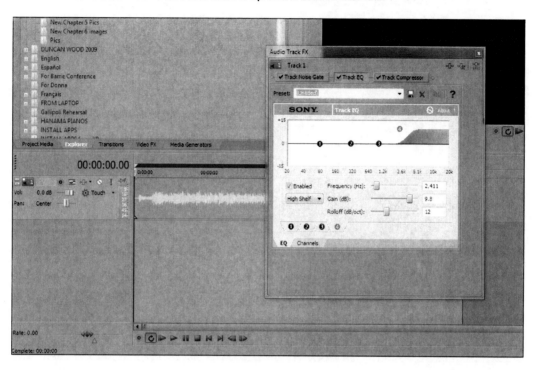

8. While you were moving the dot, you must have noticed that the **Frequency** and **Gain** parameters moved to correspond with the changes you made to the number **4** dot. As the drop box to the left of the **Gain** parameter suggests, this EQ band is currently a **High Shelf** EQ, which means that it affects the frequencies above the frequency selected.

9. If we now slide the **Roll Off** parameter, you will notice that the steepness of the curve going up to the shelf increases or decreases. The **High Shelf** EQ is similar to the **Treble EQ** setting on your home/car stereo or music device.

10. If we now change the drop-down menu from **High Shelf** to **Band** you will see that the Band EQ only affects a particular frequency with either more or less frequencies on either side of the selected frequency, dependent upon the bandwidth parameter.

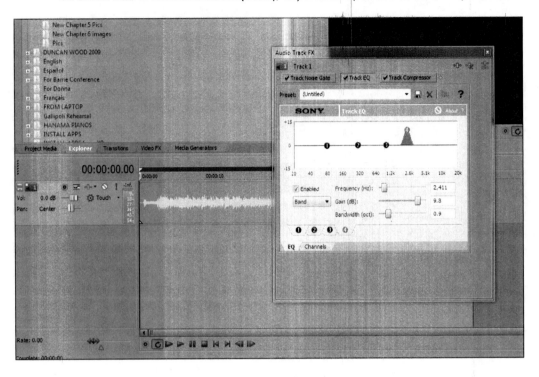

11. If you want to slide the dot and only change the **Gain** more accurately, hold the *Ctrl* button while moving the dot and it will lock the mouse vertically. To move only the **Frequency**, hold *Ctrl + Shift* to lock the mouse horizontally. The band type of EQ is similar to the mid EQ on your home/car stereo or music device.

12. The third type of EQ is **Low Shelf**, which is the same as the **High Shelf** except that it changes the frequencies below the selected frequency. This EQ is similar to the bass EQ on your home/car stereo or music device.

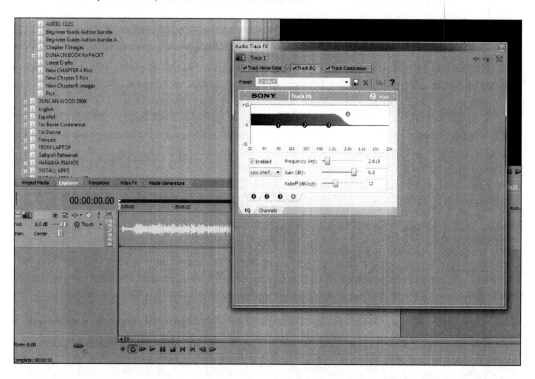

13. All four of the bands in our **Track EQ** can be changed to any of these three types of EQ. The choice is yours to suit your creative taste. One good rule of thumb to use is that subtractive EQ is often a better way to go than additive EQ, which means there are two ways to make a sound brighter. One is to add high frequencies and the second is to remove lower frequencies and turn the overall volume up. This second method is called **subtractive EQ**, although adding a touch of top end can suit certain sounds better. Also, if you aren't using a particular band in your EQ, it can help your system resources to uncheck the **Enabled** box to turn that particular band off.

14. Just like our video plugins, there are preset settings in the **Preset** drop-down menu where you can also save your favorite EQ settings.

15. One of the main things to be aware of is that certain sounds don't contain all the available frequencies, so if you had a low bass sound and you were adjusting the high shelf EQ around 15 kHz, then you probably are not going to hear any difference to the sound as the bass sound won't have much in it above 10 kHz.

What just happened?

We have now studied and made ourselves familiar with the available settings of the **Track EQ** plugin. So let's now try out these settings on our **Acc Guit** Media Clip.

Now that we have the acoustic guitar (**Acc Guit**) audio clip on the timeline, let's double click the clip to create a loop section. Turn on the loop playback by selecting *Ctrl+Shift +L* and hit the space bar to play back our selection. While it is playing, manipulate the EQ parameters to listen to what they do and try to adjust the acoustic guitar's **Track EQ** to a sound that you like. Once you have a setting you like, don't forget to save the project and also save the EQ setting into a new preset called **Acc Guit**. While you are making changes, a good way to hear the difference between the raw guitar and your new EQ setting is to un check the **Track EQ** to hear it raw and then re check it to hear the new EQ.

Compression

There is an old saying in the music business and that is "Compression Is Your Friend!" Having said that, you have to be careful not to use too much compression and the best way to do that is to truly understand what it does.

In the early days of recording audio, the only way one could adjust the levels of a recorded track was to move the microphone closer on the quiet moments and further back on the louder ones. Much in the same way a live singer will move his microphone closer to his mouth when singing quietly and pulling it away from his mouth when hitting the big notes. Of course this is handy as the singer knows when he is getting loud or quiet. As a recording engineer, it is almost impossible to know when sounds will be loud or quiet, so a tool was needed that could adjust those levels automatically, thus the birth of the audio compressor.

As its name suggests, it squashes the signal down so that it isn't as dynamically loud as before, but there is also a selection of parameters to help make the compressor work in a way that doesn't overly affect the sound, unless of course that is what you want it to do.

Time for action – using the Compressor plugin to change an audio clip

Let's use the compression plugin on our audio to see and hear how this plugin works:

1. Getting back to our audio tutorial project, let's select the **Track Compressor** plugin that is already on our **Track FX** of the **Acoustic Guitar** track by clicking on its tab.

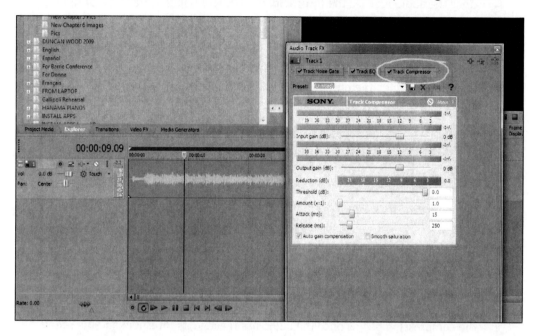

2. The **Track Compressor** plugin has several parameters, so let's apply some presets to our Acoustic guitar and point out what is happening.

3. From the **Preset** drop-down menu select **[Sys] 6:1 compression starting at -12 dB**.

4. Set up our playback loop once again and play the **Acc Guit** track, and while playing, select and de-select the **Track Compressor** plugin to hear the difference. Also watch the different VU meters on the plugin itself too.

5. Next to most of the parameters and the VU meters you will notice the symbol **dB**, which stands for decibel and is a measurement of volume. In a similar way that a millimeter is a measurement of length, a decibel is a measurement of volume.

6. While the track is playing click on the threshold slider and slide to the left. You will see that the **Reduction** VU will increase from the right. This is showing us how much the level is being reduced. The **Threshold** is basically telling the compressor to only start affecting the audio once it reaches a certain preset volume. So if the volume of the audio at any given point in time doesn't reach that volume, the compressor doesn't affect the audio.

7. Once the audio reaches the threshold, it starts to compress the audio or reduce the volume. The amount of reduction is determined by the **Amount (x:1)** parameter and is expressed as the ratio of input level above the threshold, is to level at the output of the compressor. So if the amount is set to 2.0 it is reducing the volume by 2 dB for every dB the level goes above the threshold. For example, if the level is 6 dB above the threshold then the output of the compressor would only increase by 3 dB. If the amount was set to 6.0 or 6.1 then a 6 dB increase would result in a 1 dB increase at the output so it starts to really compress the audio. Sometimes the reduction is so great that it actually makes the output a little too quiet so you have to increase the output level. To help make this easier, there is an **Auto gain compensation** function, which can be turned on or off by selecting the function at the bottom left of the plugin. This will automatically increase the output volume of the compressor if needed. Even though the **Auto gain compensation** is switched on you can still fine tune the output level with the output slider.

8. The **Smooth Saturation** switch lowers the amount of distortion created by applying heavy compression. When this parameter is turned on it reduces the "pumping" and "breathing" effect that often happens with heavy compression.

9. The last two parameters are **Attack** and **Release**. They define the speed at which the compression begins once the audio has reached its threshold and the speed at which it stops compressing once the level drops below the threshold again. For audio, such as drums, or percussive sounds, the **Attack** and **Release** would be set to faster/lower amounts.

10. While the track is playing, manipulate the parameters and try different presets to see how they affect the acoustic guitar sound. If you are unsure what setting you like, I would use the **[Sys] 6:1 compression starting at -12 dB** preset but lower the **Threshold** to around **-16.1** dB.

What just happened?

We just applied the **Track Compressor FX** to the acoustic guitar audio track and discussed the **Noise Gate** plugin to discover how their parameters effect what we are hearing. A good understanding of the **Track Compressor** plugin is essential to achieve great audio for your projects. Please read this section again a few times and play with the parameters to help you to gain a better understanding of this powerful tool.

Noise Gate

The **Track Noise Gate** plugin is a close cousin to the **Track Compressor** in that it has three of the same parameters in **Threshold, Attack,** and **Release**. The difference being that instead of compressing the tracks, audio is either muted or allowed to play depending on the volume of the track. So if the volume is loud enough it will push the gate open and the audio can be heard, but if it isn't louder than the threshold, then the gate is closed and you can't hear the audio. This is a very useful plugin if you are dealing with things, such as a reporter or dialogue that is being spoken in a noisy environment, so that when the person stops speaking the gate shuts and stops the background noise spilling into the main mix of the sound. To hear the effects of the plugin select the **Preset [Sys] Noise gate 1** and adjust the **Threshold** to around **-14.6** dB. You will hear the gate opening and shutting around the guitar as it reaches different levels.

We won't be needing this plugin on the guitar, so once you have finished playing with it, just uncheck it in the **Audio Track FX** window.

Don't forget to save our project as we go once you are happy with your settings.

Pop quiz – on the Audio Track FX

1. Which of the 3 pre inserted plug-ins on the Audio Track FX is best used to get rid of High Frequencies from an Audio Clip?
    a. The Track Noise Gate
    b. The Track Compressor
    c. The Track EQ
    d. The Screech remover

2. If the Ratio of a Track Compressor is set to 10:1, and the level increases 20 dB above the threshold, what would the increased volume at the output be?
    a. -20 dB
    b. 2 dB
    c. 0.5 dB
    d. doobee doobee dB

Have a go hero – using the Track FX on multiple tracks

Go ahead and import all of the audio clips for our audio tutorial onto their own track in the timeline. Make sure they are all hard to the left against the track header and you will be able to apply the **EQ**, **Compression**, and **Gate** if needed, onto the variety of sounds. Remember you can also mute each track on the track header as well as adjust the volume and pan parameters. Once you have them all imported to the timeline, play the track and you will hear that the files are playing back the last chorus of the song from our video tutorial project. Have some fun with creating a mix of the different sounds and make sure you use the **Compressor**, **EQ** volume and **Pan** of each track. It will be one of the best ways to learn how to apply the **Track FX** plugins. Remember one thing that I always say—*There are really no rules, just results*.

The mixing console

Although Vegas Pro 11 is primarily designed to be a video editing program, the mother company SONY has some of its roots in the music and recording industries. Because of this, Vegas Pro 11 has some very powerful and well thought out audio tools for both recording and mixing. You could in fact use the Vegas program to record and mix the audio for your project from a full music production to simple voice over dialogue. The centerpiece of these audio tools is the mixing console.

So far we have been looking at our audio tools via the same method as we deal with video, but now we will put our audio engineer hat on and look at audio from a studio engineer's perspective.

Time for action – using the mixing console

Knowing the mixing console in your software will help you to create powerful audio for your video project. Some say that audio is 70 percent of the video's quality. Let's learn how to use it here:

1. Lets access the mixing console for our audio tutorial project by using *Ctrl + Alt + 6.*

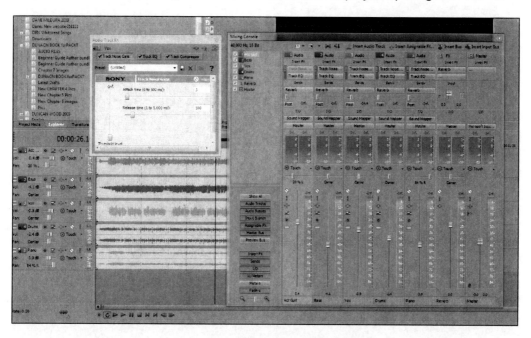

2. At first glance it can seem a little daunting with all these buttons and switches in front of you, but in reality we have just five channels (one for each audio clip) all with the same set of parameters and one master channel. To make our learning a little easier, let's turn off all the channel strips except for the first channel.

3. In the top left corner or our **Mixing Console** window, you will see the numbers of the channels with a check box beside them. Uncheck them all except for channel 1, so it looks like the following screenshot:

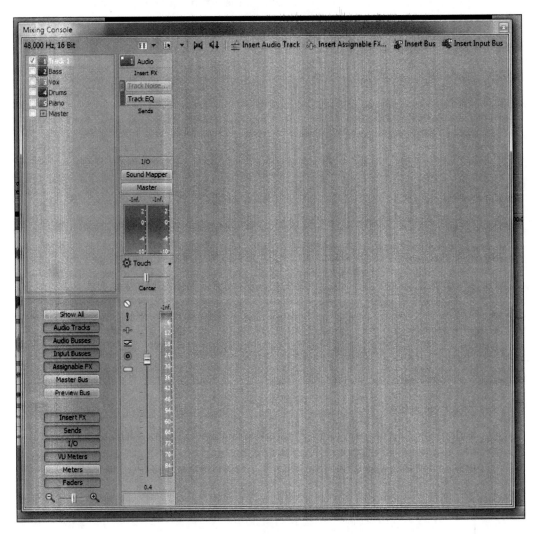

4. In the box at the bottom left of the **Mixing Console** window make sure you have the same tabs turned on and off as I do so that our consoles match.

5. Now starting at the top of the channel strip we can make our way down and identify each parameter.

6. At the top, the channel is identified with a number and the type of channel it is. In this case **Channel 1** and **Audio Track**.

7. The next section down is the **Track FX** inserted on that channel. If there are more plugins inserted than can be currently seen, you can reveal them by moving your mouse to the line just above the word **Sends** and clicking/dragging the line lower to reveal all the plugins inserted, as shown in the following screenshot:

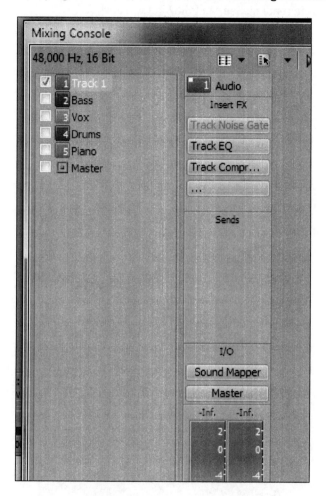

8. The next section is the **Sends** section which is currently empty. This will be used for creating an audio send which is used in the same way as an FX Send found on mixing consoles.

9. The next section is the **I/O** or input/output device. This will look at what audio interfaces and soundcards you may have attached to or installed in your computer and allow you to route audio both in and out of Vegas Pro 11 for recording and playback. The top box is the input option and the second box says **Master** which is the output assignment.

10. Below this we have the VU meters, which in the old days were called a standard volume indicator. This was shortened to VU as you could view the volume. These VU meters are more accurate than the green level meters beside the volume slider. Just as we resized the **Track FX**, we can resize the VU section to see more of the VU for a more accurate reading. See the following screenshot.

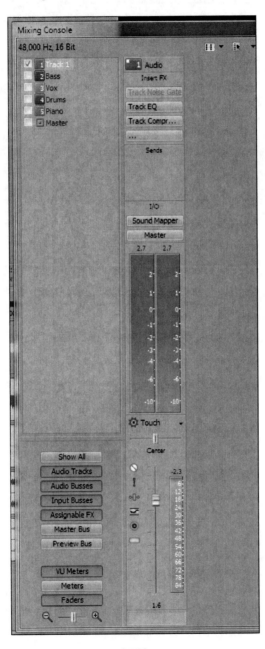

11. The next parameter is the automation setting which allows us to record our volume, panning, and mute settings in real time and play them back. The options in the drop-down menu are **Automation Off, Automation Read, Automation Write (touch), and Automation Write (Latch).** To automate our movements we simply select **Automation Write (touch)** and while the track is running, we touch the volume, pan, or mute parameters. Our movements will be recorded and played back on the next pass. The latch function is used to make edits to our previously recorded movements so that once we let go of the volume slider it will automatically return to its previous position at that point in time. More on this later.

12. The slider below the automation is the pan function, which moves our channel from either left or right in the stereo image.

13. Below this is our volume slider with all the same icon buttons down the left side as our track header. It is located to the left of the Vegas Pro 11 main timeline and includes **Mute, Solo, Insert FX, Phase, Arm for Record**, and **Input monitor Mode**.

14. At the very bottom of the channel strip is the naming box. By double-clicking on this we can enter the name of the track. My first track was the acoustic guitar so I have named it accordingly. Now recheck all the audio track's content to ensure that your track names match the sounds that are on the channels like I have done in the following screenshot:

15. Across the very top of the **Mixing Console** window there are several functions available. The top-left corner tells us the sample rate and bit depth of our audio in this session, which will match our project properties.

16. To the right of that is the **Views** tab, which changes what we see in the left-hand vertical box next to the mixer.

17. Next is the **Properties and Layout** tab for easy access to change the project parameters if we wish to. Although it is a good idea to have these set before we start the project.

18. To the right of that are the **Downmix Output** and **Dim Output** tabs. **Downmix Output** sums the stereo image into a mono playback so we can check the mix for any phase issues. The **Dim Output** allows us to turn the output down quickly and by a large amount without changing any of our master or channel volume sliders. The **Dim Output** is very handy in case the phone rings or you need to talk to someone in your studio control room while you are bouncing down or playing audio.

19. The next four icons allow us to insert four different objects—a new **Audio Track**, a new **Assignable FX**, **Insert Bus**, and an **Insert Input Bus**.

20. The new audio track is self explaining, so let's click on **Insert Assignable FX**.

21. The **Plugin chooser** window will open up showing us the various FX available. For this example, let's choose **Express FX Reverb**. Double-click to activate it and then hit **OK**.

22. You will now see that a new horizontal volume slider has appeared on each channel with **Express FX** written above it. a new FX channel strip has been created next to the master volume slider. In the assignable **Assignable FX** window let's choose the **Plate** reverb from the **Room Type** drop-down menu and push the right-hand reverb percentage all the way up to 100 percent.

23. Now if we play the project from the beginning we can slide the **Express FX** slider to the left on the vocal channel to add reverb to the voice, or to any or all the channels we like. Give it a try. The following screenshot was a capture while the project was playing to show you the levels in action and the reverb responding to our reverb send changes.

24. The **Insert Bus** icon inserts a new bus onto our mixer that we can use for a variety of functions, such as, grouping a few channels together and sending them to one bus so that their group volume can be controlled by one slider. This can be very handy in situations where you have a large group of harmony vocal tracks or multiple stringed instruments all playing at the same time. Rather than having to turn each channel up or down for say eight string players, we can send all eight strings to an **Insert Bus** and the volume of all eight channels will be controlled by the single bus track.

25. Let's insert an **Insert Bus** and then group the drums and bass together by sending them to the bus. As you can see in the following screenshot we have inserted **Bus A** that appears to the right of our reverb, and then changed the output parameter for the **Drums** and **Bass** channels to **Bus A**. Now while the project is playing we can turn the **Drums** and **Bass** up or down at the same time by using the volume of **Bus A**. We can even mute the **Drums** and **Bass** by using the **Mute** button of the **Bus A** channel. See the following screenshot and give it a try:

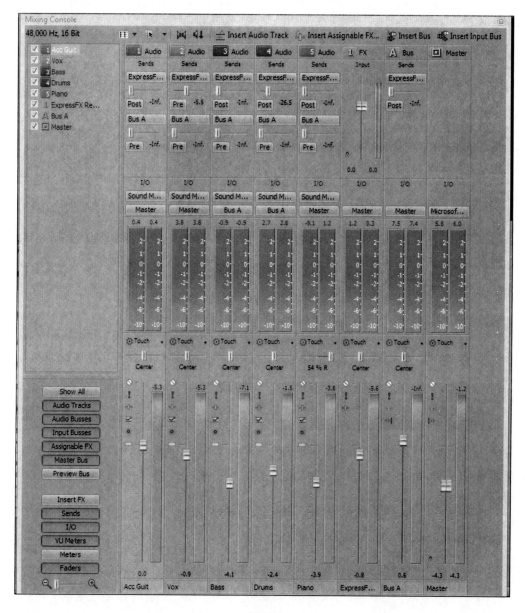

26. Lastly is the **Insert Input Bus** that allows us to bring a sound source from outside of the project into the mixer. For example, a CD player or even a microphone could be used to do a real-time narration of the video as you watch it. The configuration of the ins and outs of the mixer and the **Input Bus** is totally dependent on the hardware attached to your computer.

27. Now that you have had a good introduction to the parameters of the mixing console, spend a little time playing with the mix of our instruments again. This time use the controls of the mixing console to create a final mix.

What just happened?

The mixing console in Sony Vegas Pro 11 is a very powerful audio tool. Just as in the physical world, the mixing console in a studio is the central control system for a recording studio. The **Mixing Console** window in Vegas Pro holds the same degree of power. This section helped us get to know the mixing console and how we can use it to achieve world class audio results right from within the Vegas Pro 11 environment.

Summary

If you have never had to deal with audio and mixing consoles, then a lot of the topics covered in this chapter may seem a little alien to you. But give yourself the time to manipulate the controls to really get a good understanding of how they affect the sounds.

Once you feel you have a good grasp of the concepts we have discussed get ready to move on to learn more about audio for vision in the next chapter.

9
Soundtrack of our Lives: Audio for Video

The audio component of any video or film is a very important one indeed. Just as we have seen a language develop in the Video world, a complex language exists for us in the Audio world, when it is attached to vision. Often, a high pitch string sound is used to create a feeling of tension or that something is about to happen. The infamous two note low string stab, warned us of the impending shark attack in the movie Jaws. Musical scores or motifs have become an integral part of the video experience.

In this chapter, we shall look at some of the important factors surrounding audio and music in film and video:

- ◆ Recording the spoken word
- ◆ Microphones
- ◆ Recording a voice-over into Vegas Pro 11
- ◆ Music copyright
- ◆ Creating original music with free products such as Sony's Acid Express
- ◆ Surround sound concepts and Vegas Pro

So let's get on with it...

Recording the spoken word

As a Videographer, one of the first things you may attempt to do with audio is to record the spoken word. Whether it is an on-location camera shoot or a post production voice-over, having a strong knowledge of how to best capture and present this seemingly simple task will hold you in good stead, and make your videos a cut above the rest.

Microphones

Often the only encounter most people have with microphones is either in their mobile phone mouthpiece or chatting with their friends online with a web camera. These microphones do their job very well, but to create a professional sounding voice recording, an appropriate microphone is needed.

There are different types of microphones which generally fall into two categories:

1. Dynamic microphone

2. Condenser microphone

Dynamic microphones are very commonly used microphones in live situations such as speeches and presentations. One of the most well known dynamic microphones is the **SHURE SM58**, which is used by most singers and also at venues where the spoken word is important.

The SM58 microphone is a good all rounder, particularly in a live environment as it helps to reject handling noise when holding it. It also is optimized for both the spoken and singing voice, accentuating those sweet frequencies to capture the best quality voice from speakers.

A dynamic microphone uses a simple design with few moving parts. As well as voice, they are also better suited to handling high volume levels, such as from certain musical instruments or amplifiers. They have no internal amplifier and do not require batteries or external power.

As you may recall from your school science, when a magnet is moved near a coil of wire an electrical current is generated in the wire. Using this electromagnet principle, the dynamic microphone uses a wire coil and magnet to create the audio signal.

The diaphragm is attached to the coil. When the diaphragm vibrates in response to incoming sound waves, the coil moves backwards and forwards past the magnet. This creates a current in the coil which is channeled from the microphone along wires. A common configuration is shown in the following diagram:

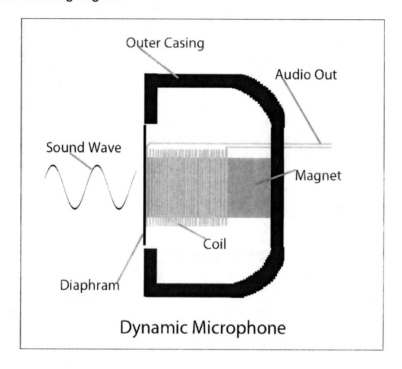

Dynamic Microphone

Condenser Microphones work in a slightly different but similar way to the dynamic microphone. A classic condenser mic is the Neuman U87 microphone seen in the next screenshot:

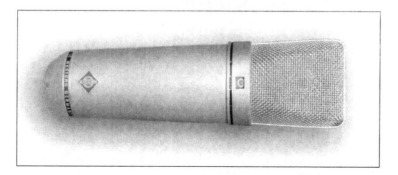

The word *condenser* means *capacitor*, a component that stores energy in the form of an electrostatic field.

Condenser microphones require power from a battery or external source. The audio signal is a stronger than that from a dynamic microphone. Condenser microphones also tend to be more responsive and sensitive than dynamic microphones, which make them well-suited to capturing subtle nuances in a sound or especially the spoken word.

The condenser microphone has two plates with a voltage between them, and one of these plates is made of very light material and acts as the diaphragm. When struck by sound waves, the diaphragm vibrates, which changes the distance between the two plates and therefore changes the capacitance. When the plates are closer together, a charge current occurs and when the plates are further apart, a discharge current occurs.

For this process to work, a voltage is required across the capacitor. This voltage is supplied either by a battery inside the microphone or by an external power source called, **Phantom Power.** Phantom power distributes DC current through audio cables to provide power for microphones and other equipment that require it. This is usually between 12 and 48 Volts, with 48V being the most common voltage used. Individual microphones draw as much current from this voltage as is needed to operate them.

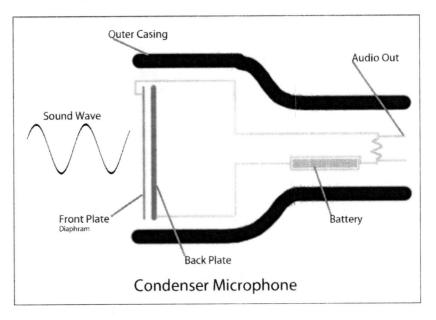

Condenser Microphone

The dynamic and condenser microphones can both be used to record a voice-over for a video project or to record live to camera. The dynamic microphone is best suited to noisy live environments and the condenser microphone is the best option for studio or quiet environments. The biggest issue of course is that, unless your camera or editing computer has a professional interface to plug the XLR lead into it, then getting the audio into the camera at the live present or into your computer in your editing space will need a small mixer or pre amp of some sort. At the very least you could use your inbuilt webcam microphone to record some voice-over audio while you are editing, but try to keep the room as quiet as possible and get as close as you can to the actual microphone to keep the direct sound strong.

Today technology has made the process of location and studio recording into computers even easier with USB microphones. There is even a condenser mic released by *IK Multimedia* called the **iRig** that you can plug straight into your **iPhone** or **iPad** and use that as a recorder, then import and re align your audio in Vegas Pro 11. That software even has 4 or 8 tracks available depending on your device to create a multi-track environment.

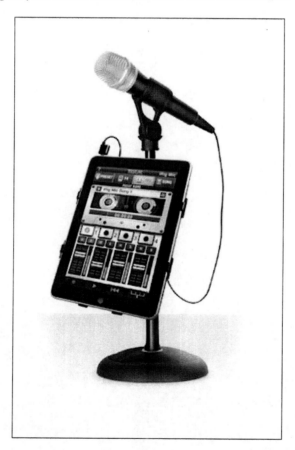

Recording a voice over into Vegas Pro 11

Regardless of your setup, which will include anything from a webcam microphone right through to a condenser microphone entering your video editing computer via a small mixer or pre amp, the process and the software application will be pretty much the same. For this exercise, I am simply using a Logitech C910 HD web camera with its built in microphone, which I will use to record some voice-over. Due to the virtually infinite number of setups you may have as your recording hardware, you will need to do some homework or talk to the people where you purchased your microphone and equipment from in order to ensure you are getting a signal from the microphone into the computer audio inputs.

Time for action – recording audio into Vegas Pro 11

As we won't be keeping this tutorial for any other purposes you can go ahead and create a new project and call it **Recording**.

1. In your new project create an audio track on the timeline.

2. Press *Ctrl + Alt + 6* to open up the Mixing Console. The console should have just a master track and the audio track you just created. See the next screenshot:

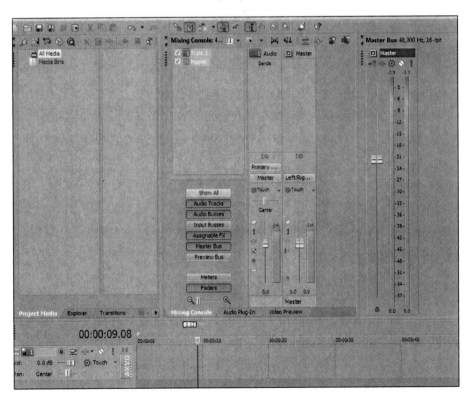

3. Under the **Options** menu select the last heading called **Preferences**, select the **Audio Device** tab, and make sure the **Audio Device Type** is set to suit your computer's soundcard or audio input card. In my case I have selected **Microsoft Sound Mapper** as I am using the web camera's microphone for the purpose of this exercise, which is plugged into the computer via USB. Hit **OK** once completed:

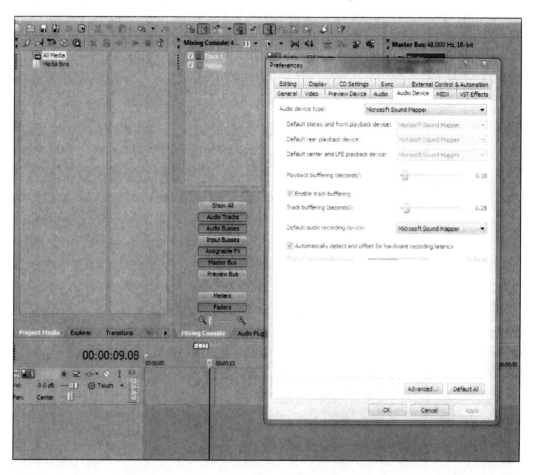

4. On our audio track in both the mixer and the timeline header you will see a little red circle that looks like a target. This is your **Record Arm** icon which puts the track into **Ready to Record** mode. Make sure your speakers are turned down a bit before selecting this Record Arm button as you may get a feedback loop that could possibly damage your speakers. Ideally do this process using headphones plugged into the headphone socket of your computer. That way your voice won't come out of the speakers and back into the microphone again, creating a roomy sound on your recording. When selecting headphones for this purpose, try to use closed back headphones so that the sound of the headphones itself doesn't feed back into the microphone. The headphones will also allow you to hear yourself better when speaking.

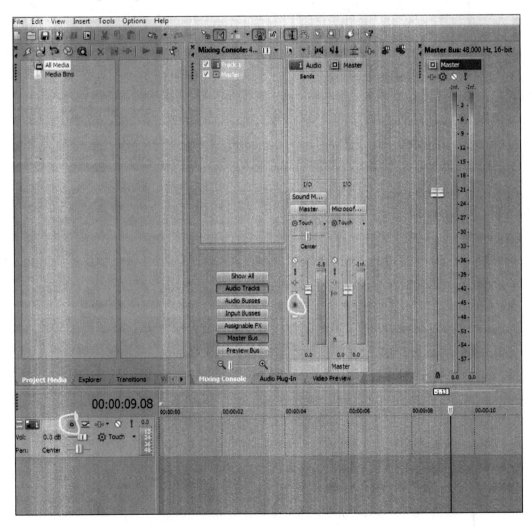

5. Once your speakers are turned down nearly all the way, or totally off if you are using headphones (in which case have the headphone volume as loud as you like to have it), click on the Record Arm button (*Ctrl + Alt + R*) and you should see some activity in the VU meter. Try saying something into your microphone and if it is connected correctly the VU meter should move up and down to your voice. If not, check all your settings according to how you were told to by the person you purchased the microphone from.

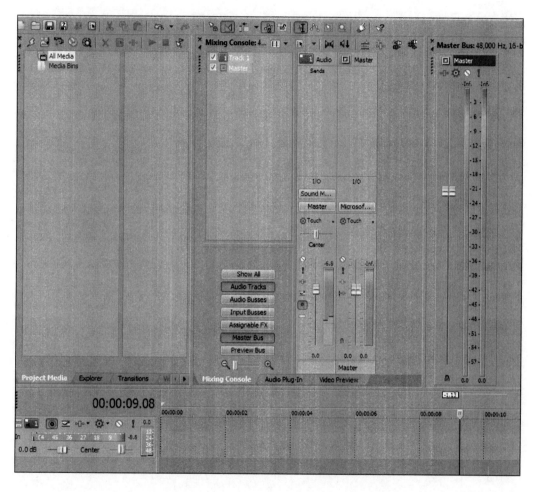

6. Once you have level coming in, make sure it isn't peaking all the way to the top of the VU meter continuously. Occasionally is okay, but not always slammed against the top as this will result in a distorted signal.

7. Play your project and once you are ready, press *Ctrl + R* to drop the project into record and say a few words such as *Testing 1 2 3*. Once finished hit **stop** or the *spacebar*.

8. An audio media clip will appear on the timeline showing the waveform of what you just said. In my case you will notice that the audio has two lines of waves as my microphone in my webcam is a stereo microphone. If you are using a mono microphone, you may only see one set of waves or two sets with one being a flat line and the other being waves that will only play out of one channel. If you hit play again it will play back and you will hear yourself speaking.

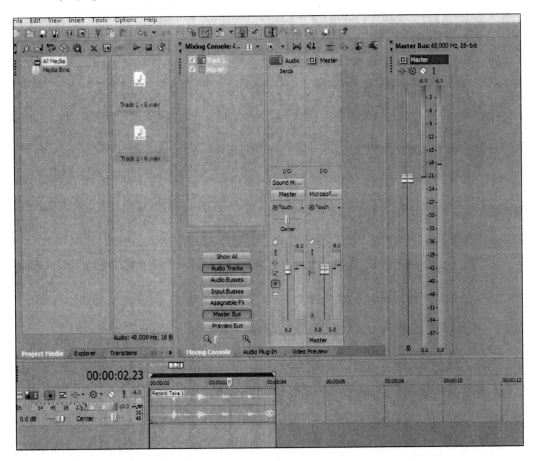

9. During playback you will notice that the Master VU meter responds to your voice as the audio is now being sent to the **Master Bus** and out of the speakers (or headphones). If it is on one side, you can change the input of the channel to only see the left or right side by changing the I/O to either **Left** or **Right**:

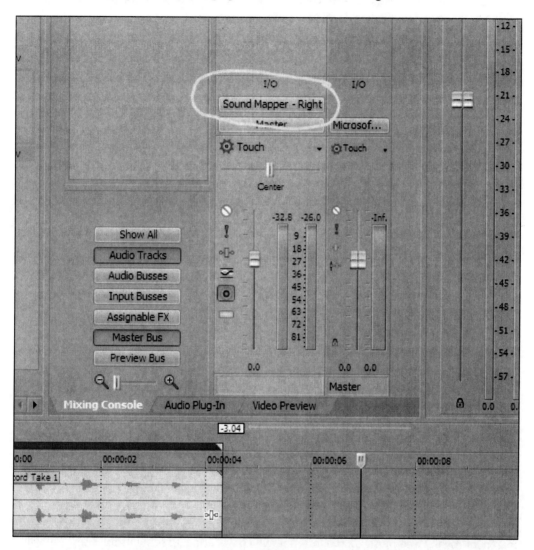

10. If you had video on the timeline, you could use this as your timing cues to place your voice over into the right positions, but if you get it wrong, it is easy to delete the audio clip and do it again or simply slide and adjust its position to suit your vision. You can now add Track FX plugins to EQ and/or compress the audio as discussed in our previous chapter.

What just happened?

We just successfully recorded some voice-over audio into Vegas Pro 11 using our microphone of choice and the mixing console within Vegas Pro 11. Armed with the knowledge you now have about microphones and the process, your video voice-over work will take your video editing projects to a whole new level of quality.

Have a go hero – creating an atmosphere with music and voice

Using our current recording project, import some instrumental music to a stereo audio track. On a separate track, record your voice by reciting poetry or simply reading some text from any book you like, but read the text in a way that suits the music you have chosen. Adjusting the voice over to suit the dynamics and pace of the music is a very important technique that will add a very professional edge to any project you are working on. Better still, find a voice-over artist who can come in to your editing setup and show you how they would deliver a piece of text and you will be amazed at the difference this makes.

Music copyright

In this the age of digital downloads and peer-to-peer networks, the music copyright issue has been raging for some time, and in that frenzy a lot of the Actual Laws and rules have become blurred. I don't mean the rules that some people think are right, I mean the actual rules applying to the ownership of vision and in particular audio and music.

When creating a video project, please note that you can't just use any piece of music you like or have in your CD collection without the prior permissions and agreement of the owner of that music. The owner can range from the songwriter through to a publishing company that owns the rights to that music. If you are just making a video to have for yourself then no problem, but as soon as you want to put it into the public domain, such as on YouTube, Vimeo, or any video sharing site, then permission is needed. Even if you aren't making any money from the video project you still need permission. A lot of people making videos or slide shows of their favorite things think they are doing the song a favor by using it in their project, but the reality is the owner of the music has the right to choose who or what their music is associated with. Sometimes the owner will be more than happy to let you use it, and other times he may not. That's their right, so the alternative is to create your own. Don't worry if you aren't musically gifted, as there are many options for you. You could also do a search for royalty free music on the Internet, which will bring up some useful sites. You will still need to pay a small fee for licensing, but anything worth using will have a cost attached.

Creating original music with products such as ACID Music Studio

Sometimes collaborating with a musician friend can bring great results to your project, but there are also software packages such as Sony's ACID Music Studio and it's free little brother **ACID Xpress**, which you can download from `http://www.sonycreativesoftware.com/download/freestuff`. See the next screenshot of the free download section of the Sony Creative Software website:

While you are there get the free 8-packs, which contain many and varied, drums, percussion, and musical instrument loops that you can manipulate in ACID Xpress to achieve some original music for your project.

Even though I am a composer and musician, sometimes a project's budget or timeframe doesn't allow for the creation of a full composition from scratch, so in these projects I often use ACID Music Studio. ACID Music Studio or ACID Pro and ACID Xpress are all very powerful audio software packages that use a lot of the functionality of the audio engine within Vegas Pro 11, and then some.

All in all using software such as these titles will give you an even greater sense of achieving a fully original project including your own sound and vision.

Surround sound concepts and Vegas Pro

Lastly, the tool that we haven't discussed so far in the audio realm of Vegas Pro 11 is the **Surround Sound Mixer** and plugins. Surround sound or 5.1 audio as it is often called, has certainly expanded its horizons in recent years, especially with the ability to store huge amounts of video and audio on Blu-ray media. The how-to and options for placement of sounds within the surround sound field are so immense that I could write a book just on that topic alone, so here we shall touch on the surround sound abilities of the Vegas Pro 11 software.

For the uninitaited, surround sound usually consists of the following channels: a front Stereo Pair, a rear Stereo Pair, a front Center Mono, and a Sub Bass Channel. The 2 Stereo Pairs and the Mono Center are the 5 channels and the Sub Bass channel gives us the **.1** of **5.1 Surround Sound**.

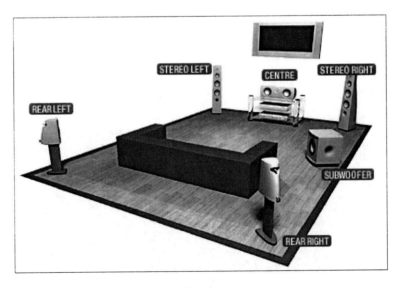

You will find that there are variations to this setup such as 7.1 and 7.2 as well as systems that have 9.1. But these versions really are just an adaptation of the 5.1 setup, which is the most common.

Time for action – using Surround Sound tools in Vegas Pro 11

To access the surround sound tools we have to turn them on in Project Properties.

1. Create a new project and call it **Surround**.

2. Open **Project Properties**. Press Alt + *Enter*.

3. Choose the **Audio** tab.

4. In the **Master Bus Mode** setting, select **5.1 surround** and hit **Apply**.

5. You will now see that the **Master Bus** window has Stereo Front Pair Channels, Stereo Rear Pair channels, a Center Mono channel, and **Low Frequency Effects (LFE)** Mono channel:

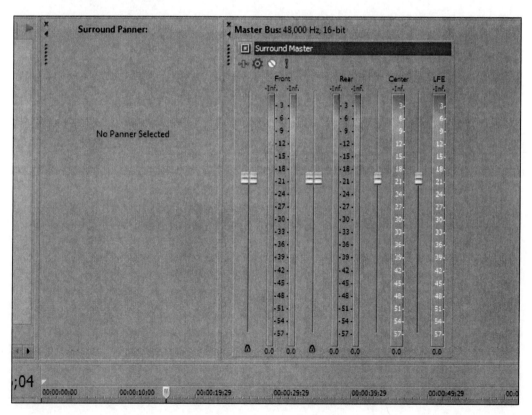

6. On the timeline, create an audio track and you will see that it has a **Surround Panner** on the Track header. (Circled in Red in the next screenshot). Click on this Panner and a large version will appear in the **Surround Panner** window. If the Surround Panner window isn't open, press *CTRL + ALT + 3* to access it.

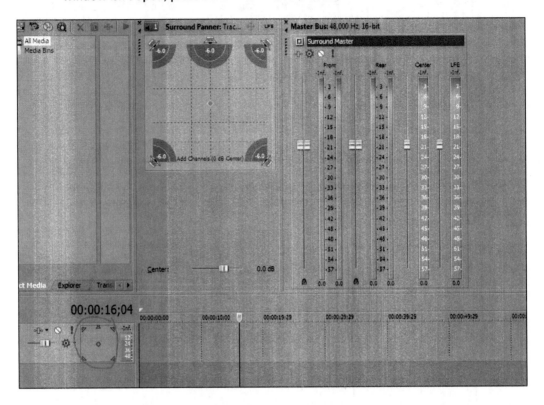

7. If you study the Surround Panner closely, you will see that it has five speakers on it, one in each corner to represent the Front and Rear Stereo Pairs and the Front Center. By clicking and holding the **Dot** in the middle of the **Surround Panner**, you can send the audio on that track to any of those speakers or to a combination of them. For example, the sound of a police car siren coming from in front of your windscreen may start at the front centre and slowly pan towards you and then down the right side of the center of the Panner then out to the back of the right rear speaker.

8. All of these movements can be automated by using key frames as we have done for every other plugin or device. If you press *SHIFT + P*, the Automation key frames will open under the audio track. Now right-click on the **Automation Setting** icon on the track header, and from the **Automation** menu select **Show Automation Controls**. You will see that two sliders appear under the Panner as well as the key frames under the timeline, as in the next screenshot:

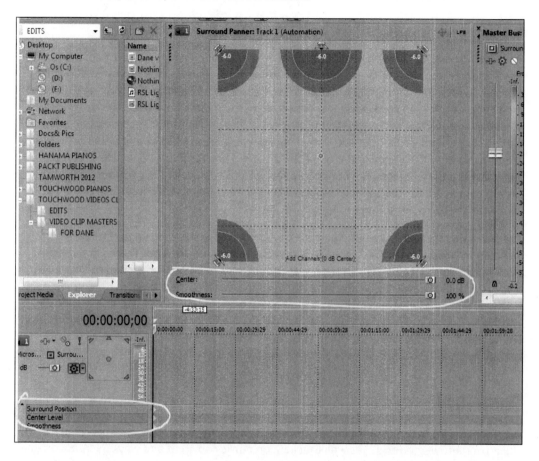

9. If you play the project (even if it's empty) and move the **Surround Panner** dot around, those movements will be recorded and on playback will move as you did. Give it a try.

10. The Center Slider adjusts the volume of the signal going to the center speaker and the Smoothness Slider affects how smoothly the automation occurs

11. As for the **LFE Channel,** back in the Project Properties under the Audio tab there is an option to turn on a **Low Pass Filter** for the LFE. This basically means if the Low Pass Filter selected is 180Hz, then any frequency below 180Hz, that is on a channel assigned to the Surround Panner, will send those low frequencies to the LFE. The various Low Pass Filter options available will vary depending on which method of Surround Sound Encoding is being used on the final Blu-ray or DVD.

What just happened?

We have just learned how to turn our project into a surround sound project and how to use and apply automation to the Surround Panner of one audio track. As you can imagine, a project with many audio tracks that all require precise surround sound panning will make for a very complex mixing experience. Action movies will often have over 100 audio tracks in play to achieve the high action sound effects such as gun battles, car chases, and war battle scenes, with virtually an audio track for every bullet, explosion, and visual component requiring sound FX being moved around the 3D audio environment. As well as these high track numbers, a listening room equipped with the equivalent 5.1 surround speaker system connected to your editing computer via a multichannel audio interface is needed to complete the surround sound mixing of your project.

There are also three 5.1 surround plugin FX available in the standard Vegas Pro 11 installation, including **Dither, Track EQ,** and **Wave Hammer Surround.** These three plugins work in conjunction with the surround settings you have selected for each particular audio track and help to make the best settings for your mixes. Of particular note is the **Wave Hammer Surround** plugin, which has a suite consisting of Compressor, Volume Maximizer, and Audio Router available for your use. As you delve deeper into the surround sound world, you will find there are many third-party surround sound audio plugins available such as spatial reverbs and delays to really enhance your projects.

Summary

We learned a lot in this chapter about the spoken word, microphones, and recording a voice-over into Vegas Pro 11, as well touching on music copyright and ways to create original music with free products such as Sony's ACID Xpress. Combining this knowledge with the surround sound abilities of Vegas Pro 11 will help you to achieve that Pro finish you are after for your video project.

Let's move forward now onto the next chapter.

10
Can I put this on YouTube?: Rendering and Delivering the Final Project

Sony Vegas Pro 11 gives the user the ability to render projects ready for many different formats and devices. From QuickTime and MPEG2 to MP4 and MP3, all these acronyms can be confusing. This chapter will help to demystify the language and allow the reader to make the right choice for delivering the final product.

In this chapter we will cover the following topics:

- Why is video digitally compressed anyway?
- What is a codec?
- Video formats and where they are mostly used
- Audio formats and where they are mostly used
- Choosing the right format
- Rendering video and audio for DVD Architect
- Rendering for the Web
- Burning DVD and Blu-ray right from the timeline
- More rendering information

Video compression

As with almost anything digital, the more bits of information available to the processing computer, the more accurate and higher quality your final product will be. This applies to both the video and audio worlds. Not that long ago, we were content with a video that had a 4:3 aspect ratio and was delivered in a small digital format of 726 x 576 pixels (PAL). But now with the advent of both HD video and high speed Internet, the formats and options are huge. The hard part is deciding which format you need to render your project to for delivery to your audience.

One of the first places you will put your final video for others to see will probably be on the Internet. Whether it is on your own website or on one of the many free available popular sites, such as YouTube. Up until recently all videos on YouTube were in the **FLV** format or **Flash Video** format. I say recently as with the introduction of the new Internet language HTML5, we shall see the FLV trend changing over to **MP4** format. Vegas Pro 11 already has a MainConcept MP4 Codec option in our Render As choices, so we are already set to supply our video in the right format for the Internet. Even if you are unsure of the format needed, thankfully sites like YouTube will convert your video into the right format to be optimized for playback. Just check which formats they will accept before the final render.

Codecs

The word codec is a portmanteau of **Compressor-Decompressor** or, more commonly, **Coder-Decoder**. Why do we have to use a codec? Simply to make the amount of data smaller, which in turn makes the video load and play faster as well as not use up too much of your precious Internet bandwidth or download allowances. A codec encodes a data stream or signal for transmission, storage, or encryption, or decodes it for playback or editing. A video camera's **Analog-to-Digital Converter (ADC)** converts its analog signals into digital signals, which are then passed through a video compressor for digital transmission or storage. A receiving device then runs the signal through a video decompressor, then a **Digital-to-Analog Converter (DAC)** for analog display. The closest format we have to film, which would be considered uncompressed, is High Definition uncompressed video, and by high definition I mean **4K** video, which if you recall from our discussions in Chapter 1, *Getting Acquainted with your New Best Friend: Vegas Pro 11 Overview*, has 4096 x 2160 pixels versus HD's 1920 x 1080 pixels. This number of pixels translates to a very large amount of 1s and 0s to digitally represent the video, which in turn means lots of hard drive space.

A recent project I was working on was shot in HD 1920 x 1080 for a 4 minute song, and the project that was storyboarded and shot took up over 2 terabytes of storage space. That's 2000 gigabytes of data. Even once edited and rendered to a master file, the data size will be too big to allow for playing back over the Internet, so a device had to be created that reduced the amount of data without losing the *quality* of the video. Thus, the birth of Lossless and Lossy codecs ensued.

These codecs reduce the data greatly while minimizing the loss in quality of the video's image. Currently one of the most popular codecs is **H.264**, which is part of the **MP4** format family.

Video formats available

If you look at the **Render As** page of Vegas Pro 11, you will discover many varied formats that you can render your final master video file into:

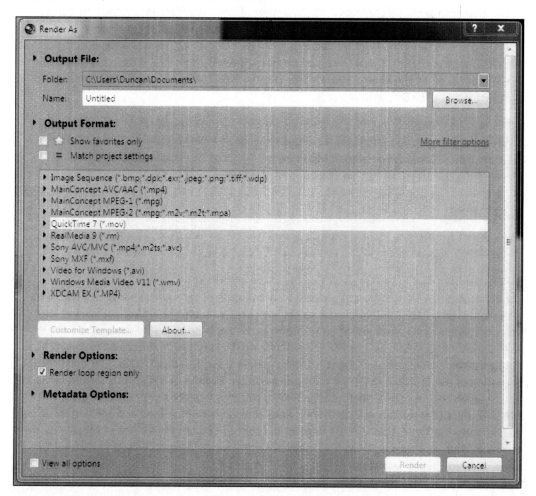

The following descriptions will help you to understand the most popular formats a little better and which ones to use for your next master video file.

Image Sequence

The Image Sequence output format creates a set of still-image files representing the source video frame-by-frame. This encoder is used to convert a video clip to an image sequence for use with compositing applications that aren't compatible with QuickTime.

AVC

AVC stands for **Advanced Video Coding** and is a part of the MPEG-4 family, which is still a developing standard and is divided into a number of parts. Unfortunately, the companies promoting MPEG-4 compatibility do not always clearly state the "part" level compatibility. The key parts we are mostly interested in are MPEG-4 part 2 (MPEG-4 SP/ASP, used by codecs such as DivX, Xvid, Nero Digital, 3ivx, and by QuickTime 6) and MPEG-4 part 10 (MPEG-4 AVC/H.264, used by the x264 codec, by Nero Digital AVC, by QuickTime 7, and by next-gen DVD formats like HD DVD and Blu-ray).

MPEG-4 is also found in 3GP files. A growing number of mobile and smart phones have a video recording option and most store their files as 3GP files (name derived from the creators, **Third Generation Partnership Project**). 3GP files can be played on QuickTime Player and RealPlayer, but not on Windows Media Player.

MPG (MPEG)

MPG stands for **Moving Picture Experts Group** (driven by Microsoft's file standard of a three-letter extension box, MPEG has evolved by dropping the "E" to become MPG).

MPG is very popular in the video world, and there are a number of MPG formats that you should consider, all with different purposes. Distribution of video on the Internet and discs was pioneered by MPG video, thus, it works with pretty much everything. MPEG-1 gives you poor video quality and in some situations, no better than VHS. The next generation of MPEG technology is MPEG-2, which is used by most TV stations. MPEG-2 technology is the compression format behind DVD, as well as a standard for broadcast HDTV. The most recent evolution of the format is: MPEG-4 (commonly known as MP4 or M4V). This format deals with a much better picture quality. MPEG-4 absorbs many of the features of MPEG-1 and MPEG-2 and other related standards, and adds support for embedded and META data. It is also streamable and supports most multimedia content. iTunes makes use of MPEG-4 with the iPod, iPad, and iPhone, as well as often being the most commonly used file format for sharing videos over the Internet.

MOV

The MOV file extension was created by Apple. MOV files are often used to store videos due to its highly efficient compression ability. There are currently several digital cameras that automatically store files in MOV format. MOV is compatible with both Windows and Mac platforms, but this file can only be played with QuickTime Player or QuickTime-compatible editing software such as Vegas Pro 11.

Real Media

RealPlayer (RP) has a specific file extension that runs exclusively on its player. RealVideo is usually paired with RealAudio and packaged in a RealMedia (. rm) container. RealMedia is suitable for use as a streaming media format that is being sent over a network. Streaming video is often used to watch live television, since it does not require downloading the video in advance.

Sony AVC

This is an MP4 codec created by Sony for the creation of content for many of the Sony products such as the PlayStation 3, PlayStation Portable, and so on.

Sony MXF

Not so much a codec but a format to help the exchange of video project sessions between different video editing software packages. Most professional editing software supports MXF and therefore allows for collaboration between various editors who are running different software packages as well as helping to make projects future proof to some degree.

AVI

The acronym **AVI** comes from **Audio Video Interleave**. AVI is a fairly simple codec, making it a go-to video format that can be played on almost any media player.

It is Considered by some to be an outdated container format due to its cumbersome application when used with popular MPEG-4 codecs (Xvid and DivX, for example), as it increases the file size more than necessary.

As AVI files also do not contain pixel aspect ratio information, the frame often appears stretched or squeezed horizontally when the file is played back. Although it has limitations, AVI is still very popular due to its compatibility with many of the popular playback engines.

WMV

WMV stands for **Windows Media Video** with a specific codec—the WMV codec. These files will only play on the Windows Media Player or RealPlayer. WMV files are arguably the most popular and widely used streaming media format on the Internet (possibly an equal tie with FLV).

XDCAM EX

This format allows for compatibility with Sony's growing range of XDCAM cameras, with Sony Vegas Pro 11 including a built in XDCAM explorer. XDCAM uses an optical media disc system that also allows the cameras and decks to operate as a VTR unit, which essentially emulates the traditional linear based workflows. The XDCAM HD optical disk format acts as both a playback and storage media.

FLV

Currently Vegas Pro 11 doesn't have a Flash Video codec to render to, but there are a few conversion programs that will allow you to create an FLV file from your final render. You've no doubt viewed a FLV file—whether you knew it or not. **FLV** stands for **Flash Video**. When you click on a web page and see a video playing on that page (whether it be an intro video, advertisement, or entertaining video), you are generally seeing an FLV in action. Flash videos use the Adobe Flash Player. You can download it for free if you don't have it from: `http://get.adobe.com/flashplayer/`.

Composed of complex codecs, Flash videos are created with a very good video quality. FLV files work well streaming over the Web and can be played by pretty much any media player created. Adobe Flash Player is practically universally accepted. This will change soon with the advent of the HTML5 Protocol. iPhones and iPads don't play FLV files, but HTML5 will fix this issue

Audio formats available

The second thing to consider when creating a master file is which **Audio Format** or **Audio Codec** you should use. Once again, in the **Render As** page of Vegas Pro 11, you will find a wide variety of audio formats to select from. To access the audio formats you need to have an audio track with some media on it and solo the audio track prior to selecting the Render As function. That way the audio formats will appear in the Render As window.

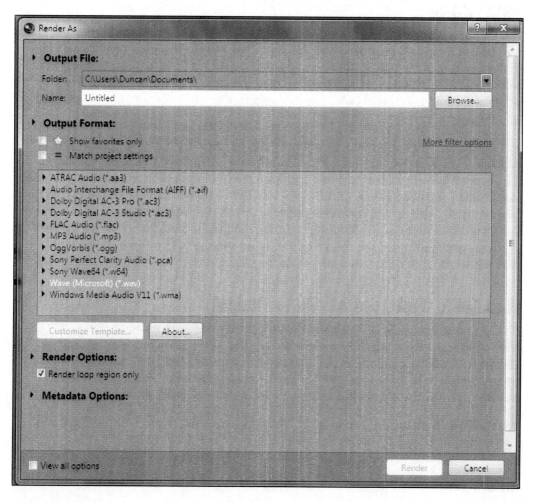

ATRAC Audio

This allows for audio compatibility with some of Sony's earlier portable audio devices such as the Memory Stick Walkman and the Sony MiniDisc player.

AIFF (Audio Interchange File Format)

AIFF is a non compressed format co-developed by Apple Computer Company and is mostly used on their MAC computers, although most audio players that play WAV files will usually play AIFF files. AIFF has the added bonus of being able to store a loop point along with the audio data and or a note on the content.

DOLBY AC-3

This format was originally used in movie theatres to play back the audio of 35 mm film where the audio was optically recorded on to the filmstrip between the perforation holes on the soundtrack side of the film. A scanner would read the data, a Dolby Digital processor would extract it as AC-3 digital audio, and then it is played back as 5.1 surround audio. The film would also carry an analogue Dolby Stereo soundtrack as a fallback in case the digital data was damaged or corrupted.

As TV broadcast, movie theater and Internet video has developed, the AC-3 codec is now available in many realms and Vegas Pro 11 caters to creating audio files in this format. AC-3 5.1 surround files are used extensively in Blu-ray and DVD production and are the most used format when authoring Blu-ray or DVDs in Sony's DVD Architect 5.2 or later. The two formats called AC-3 PRO and AC-3 Studio simply differ in that the Pro version allows for the use of Dolby metadata where as the Studio version does not. Dolby Metadata is carried within the Dolby bitstream and it controls downstream encoders and decoders by relaying precise information about the encoded audio, ready for playback.

FLAC AUDIO (Free Lossless Audio Codec)

FLAC is an open format with royalty-free licensing and a reference implementation that is free software. FLAC has support for metadata tagging, album cover art, and fast seeking. Though FLAC playback support in portable audio devices and dedicated audio systems is limited compared to formats like MP3 or uncompressed PCM, FLAC is supported by more hardware devices than competing lossless compressed formats like Wavepack.

The **European Broadcasting Union (EBU)** has adopted the FLAC format for the distribution of high quality audio over its Euroradio network.

MP3

MP3 is an audio-specific format that was designed by the Moving Picture Experts Group (MPEG) as part of its MPEG-1 standard and later extended in the MPEG-2 standard. Known as MP3, it is a commonly used format for the domestic market, especially for space critical storage and audio playback devices. As a lossy compression format there is a trade off of sound quality versus file size, but even at its highest allowable bit rate, I still find MP3 not suitable for professional audio quality even though many consumers don't mind the inferior sound.

Ogg VORBIS

Ogg is another free format that is unrestricted by software patents. This audio format is part of the Ogg container format, which can multiplex a number of independent streams for audio, video, text (such as subtitles), and metadata. Because the format is free, the Ogg codecs have been incorporated into a number of free proprietary media players, and therefore Sony have made it available to you in case you need to deliver video or audio to the Ogg formats.

Sony Perfect Clarity Audio

This audio codec was created for the Sound Forge range of audio editing software that SONY acquired in 2003. This codec is made available to the Sony Creative Software range.

Sony Wave 64

With the advent of 64-bit processing, this codec is a true 64-bit audio codec that doesn't have the file size limitation of 4 gigabytes other audio codecs may have. Particularly with 5.1 surround audio in 64-bit format, a feature film or video product could easily extend past the previously annoying file size limit.

Wave

Wave files have been the most common audio file format found on Windows PCs, but as a 32-bit file it does suffer from the limitation of the 4 gigabyte maximum mentioned in the previous format. Although a 4 GB Wave file at 44.1kHz sample rate with a 16-bit format will give you 6 hours and 45 minutes of audio, as all computers advance quickly into the 64-bit format, and the surround sound trend continues to grow, the long lived WAV file may find itself left behind. Having said that, for audio quality we have become accustomed to on CDs, this is the audio format of choice.

Windows Media Audio

Known as **WMA**, this audio data compression was developed by Microsoft and is part of the Windows Media Framework used to create Windows Media Files that will play back in the **Windows Media Player**. Created originally as a competition for MP3 and Real Audio, the format now has a newer, more advanced codec in **WMA Pro** that supports multichannel and high resolution audio.

Rendering video and audio for DVD Architect

One of the big pluses in purchasing Vegas Pro 11 is that you get the bundled **DVD Architect** authoring software for free. This software is a very powerful authoring package that allows you to create both **DVD** and **Blu-ray** discs.

For DVD discs, the format of choice to render to is the MPEG 2 format and in particular you will find already prepared DVD Architect templates ready to use.

Time for action - preparing Master Files for DVD Architect

Often the final step when creating a project is to burn the final master video to a DVD or Blu-ray. Here we will go through this process to create our final disk.

1. Open our Beginner's Guide Project. That is the music video clip.

2. Once the project has loaded, double click on the music audio clip, which will create a loop point at the beginning of the audio clip and at the end. These will be marked with small yellow flags at the top of the timeline:

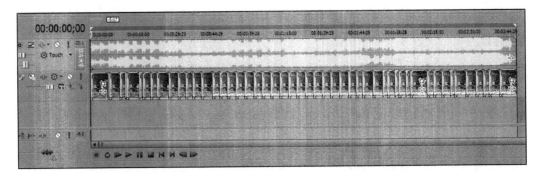

3. Select **Render As** from the **File** menu and the **Render As** page will open.

4. Click the little black arrow next to **MainConcept MPEG 2** output format to reveal the template options.

5. Here you will find **DVD Architect PAL Widescreen Video Stream**, which will have an = sign to its left. This equals sign indicates that our project properties match the format properties the best in its category.

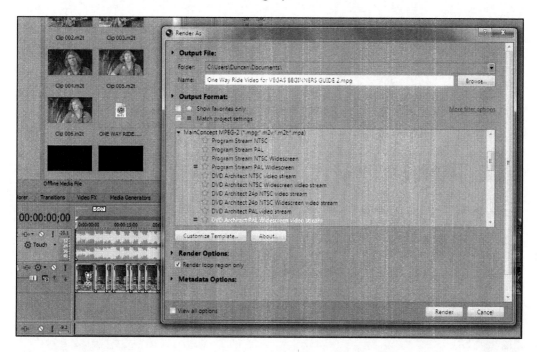

6. You will notice it says **Video Stream**, which means when it renders there will be no audio content in it. The reason we do this is that we want to keep our audio as a file with only one compression process applied to it. Therefore, it is best to allow DVD Architect to apply that compression to the audio once it is in that program rather than compress it once in Vegas Pro 11 and once again in DVD Architect.

7. By Clicking **Customize Template** we can have a look at the settings and make any adjustments we might like to apply:

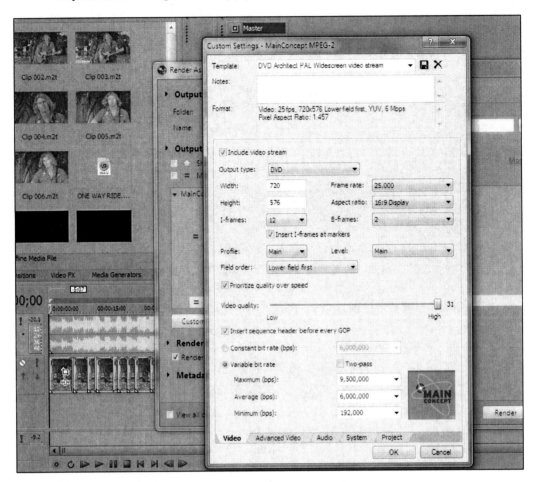

8. Here you will see that we are rendering to a **DVD** output type with a screen resolution of **720 x 576** at **25** frames per second and an **Aspect ratio** of **16:9 Display**.

9. This template is ready to go so hit **OK** and then use the **Browse** button in the **Output File** section to select where on your computer you wish to render the master file to. Give the file a name such as **One Way Ride Video**.

10. Once you have set the location and name, select the **Render** button and the rendering process will commence. The time taken to render this file will highly depend on the power of your computer.

11. A progress bar will appear with a rough estimate of how much time it will take. You will also notice that this estimated time varies as the project progresses, sometimes getting shorter and other times longer. It is only a rough estimate so you can decide whether to go make a coffee or not:

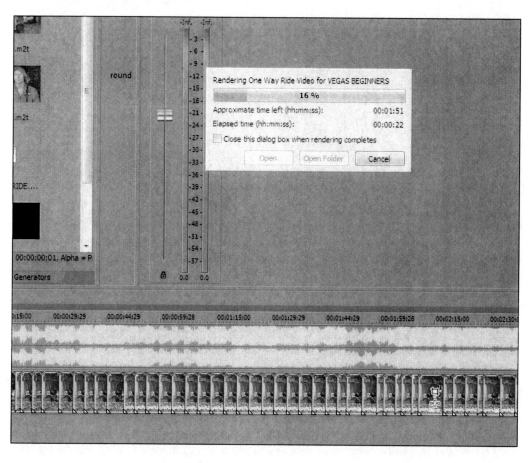

12. Once the video has finished, the progress bar will say **Render Complete**. Hit **Cancel** and we are now ready to render our audio file for the DVD.

13. Solo the audio track of our session and once again select **Render As** and our audio options will be available.

14. Select **Microsoft Wave** and choose the **44,100 16 bit Stereo, PCM** format:

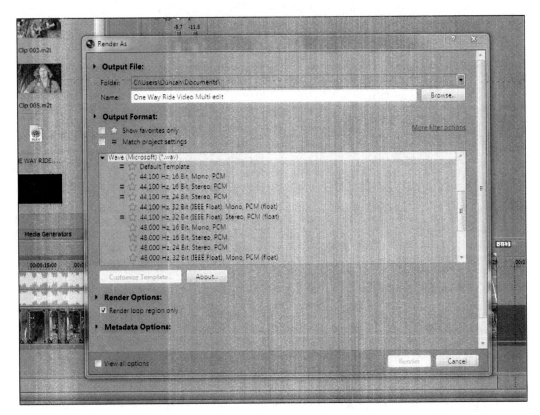

15. Make sure you save the audio render to the same folder as you did the video render and ensure it has the same name as the video render. This way when you import the video file into DVD Architect, it will import the audio file automatically for you.

16. Now click **Render**. The audio render will process very quickly as the audio format is the same as the original file, and audio renders take up very little processing power. Once we create our DVD master with DVD Architect, the audio may go through a compression process to convert it to the appropriate format for the kind of DVD you have chosen. Usually it will convert the audio to a Sony AC-3 format audio file.

17. You can now use the video and audio master files to create your DVD in **Sony DVD Architect**.

18. For Blu-ray we would follow the same process with the exception of using much higher quality High Definition video and audio formats to suit our playback media. With so much empty space available on a 50 GB recordable Blu-ray, we could use the highest resolution formats available without fear of coming anywhere near running out of space for our single Music Video Clip.

19. In our **Render As** window under the MainConcept MPEG-2 (*.mpg, *.m2v, *.mpa) format, we will find several preset Blu-ray output formats ready for you selection. Remember the higher the bitrate (that is Mbps) the larger the final file will be. See the following screenshot:

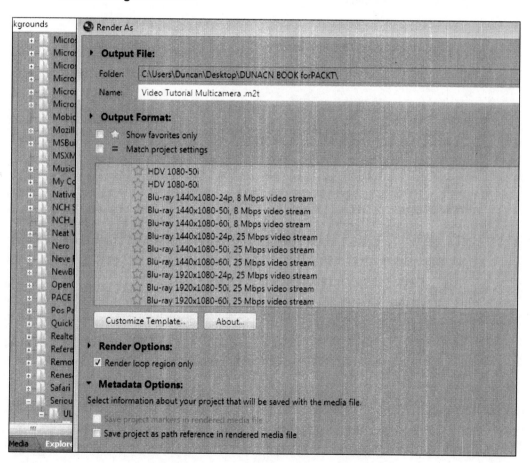

What just happened?

We just prepared both video and audio master files to use in DVD Architect to create a DVD of our final edit of our Beginners' Guide Project. This process is the same for Blu-ray creation with the difference being the video and audio formats used are of a higher resolution.

Pop quiz

1. The word codec is derived from which two words?

   a. Co Dependence

   b. Copper Decimals

   c. Compression Decompression

   d. Compassion Decreased

2. Of the many audio formats available, which one is currently the format of choice for audio CDs?

   a. WMA (Windows Media Audio)

   b. Sony Wave 64

   c. Ogg Vorbis

   d. Wave

3. When preparing video and audio files to be used in Sony DVD Architect, which of the following is the correct method?

   a. Render video and audio files at the same time

   b. Render video and audio files separately

   c. Render audio before video

   d. All of the above

Rendering for the Web

If your video is to be placed on the Web, we need to consider the best format that will be used to broadcast the media. As the Internet becomes faster and video server websites such as YouTube, Vimeo, and so on cater to high definition video delivery, our format of choice should be as high a quality as possible. Thankfully, YouTube does the final conversion to a format that is best used for its player automatically. As long as you keep your final video within the guidelines provided by YouTube, then you pretty much can't go wrong. The same applies to most of the popular video hosting websites. When rendering our master video for the Web, we would use a template that renders the video and audio at the same time so that both streams are contained in the one file. A good Render As option for this is the MainConcept AVC/AAC (*.mp4) output format. Here you will find output formats ready to go for all the Apple devices as well as the various format options used by YouTube. See the next screenshot:

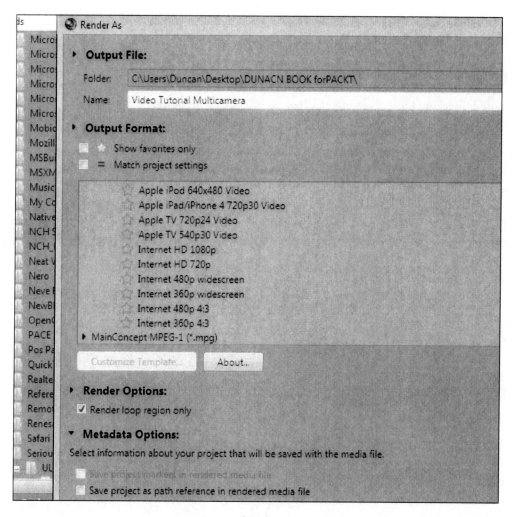

MP4 is quickly becoming the format of choice, especially with the introduction of the new HTML5 coding, which allows for your MP4 files to play on portable devices such as iPhones and iPads, which in the past wouldn't play the standard FLV Flash files.

Have a go hero

As we haven't actually worked through the process of creating a Blu-ray disk, have a go at using the rendering formats for Blu-ray video and audio to create a Blu-ray disk in DVD Architect. Remember to use the MainConcept MPEG-2 video format for Full HD 1920 x 1080 video and uncompressed Wave audio format. Even if you don't yet have a Blu-ray burner in your system, try out these settings to make it clearer in your mind as well as getting to know how long your current editing computer will take to render out a project of this size in those high quality formats.

Each time you access the Render as page, it is good to have a look at the details of each format to know what is available to you.

Burning DVD or Blu-ray directly from the timeline

Another quick method of creating a viewable disc is to burn either a DVD or Blu-ray disc directly from the Vegas Pro 11 timeline. This is a fast method to create a single-movie DVD or Blu-ray disc to share your productions. I wouldn't use this for your final product as it doesn't allow for the full pallet of authoring features available when using DVD Architect, but is a quick way to make a disc to give your client or collaborator a chance to review your stages of work on the project.

Time for action - burning a disc directly from the timeline

This tool is a great way to quickly burn a disc to give to your collaborator or client to view before you go through the process of authoring a full final DVD or Blu-ray disk.

1. With our Music Video project open, double-click the audio media clip to select our render section.

2. From the **Tools** menu, select **Burn Disc**.

3. An options menu will appear giving us the options **Track–at-Once Audio CD**,
Disk-at-Once Audio CD, **DVD**, and **Blu-ray Disc**:

4. The first two options are for creating an Audio disk. One of the selected audio tracks
on the timeline, with the other rendering out all the audio active in the project.

5. From the next two video options, select **DVD**.

6. The **Burn DVD** window will now open giving us a **Video Format** box, and an **Audio Format** box, which will be preset to the Project Properties **Audio format:**

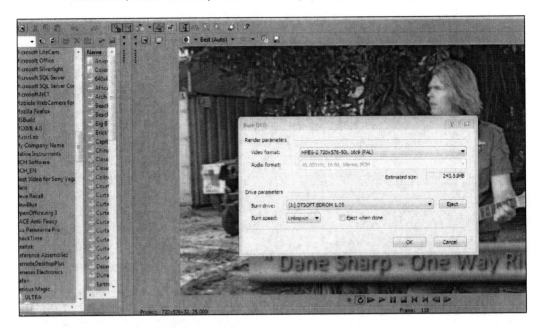

7. The video format box will be set to the **video format** that best suits our project properties translated for DVD. In this case, that is **MPEG-2 720x576-50i, 16:9 (PAL)**.

8. The video format has a drop-down option where we can select other DVD formats such as **NTSC** and the **4:3** pixel aspect ratio. This would be great if we are collaborating with a person in another region of the world or the client needs to play the DVD on a different system to yours.

9. Once you are happy with your selected video format, insert a blank DVD into your burner and hit **OK**.

10. The system will now render and burn your DVD for you.

11. The final disk is the kind of DVD that once you place it in a DVD player, it will play automatically, without any menu options.

What just happened?

We went through the process of using the Burn Disc from the timeline tool. This tool is ideal for burning either a DVD or Blu-ray disk quickly, which creates a single movie disk to share your production.

More rendering information

The rendering process, regardless of the delivery method, is pretty much the same as described in the previous *Time for action* section with the difference laying in the output video and audio property values. Having said that, we must also take care in knowing what format our final video will be needed in, right at the beginning of the shooting process. If for example, we were producing a short film or advertising segment that would be displayed at movie theaters, then we need to be very aware of the Aspect Ratio required to display the project on the big screen. Although all HD TVs today have 16:9 ratio, movie theaters have a different ratio of 1.85:1 in the USA and 1.66:1 in Europe. This isn't considered when filming commences, then some of the footage upper and lower regions will be lost such as in the following screenshot of our clip:

As you can see, this cinematic look, which is the 1.85:1 USA ratio, starts to cut into our picture top and bottom and we would have to go to each clip and adjust its Pan/Crop tool to get the most from the scene. But in general, pretty much all delivery methods such as DVD, Blu-ray, YouTube, PlayStation Video, PSP Video, HD TV, and so on, are all 16:9 aspect ratio, it is simply the bit rate of the video which will define the quality.

Obviously the higher the bitrate, the higher the quality and therefore the bigger the data amount needed to supply the whole film. This is why Blu-ray can hold up to 25 GB in a single layer disc and 50 GB in a double layer disc, to accommodate these larger files. Plus with all the behind the scenes footage and the "Making Of" content added to the Blu-ray package, these sizes are essential.

As you start to encounter other delivery methods, you will generally find a codec to suit that method. If you look at the codecs available just in the Sony AVC/MVC section of the Render As window, you will find it starts at a simple 512 kbps for showing a low quality video straight from a USB stick, up to FULL HD 16 mbps for Blu-ray, and everything in between.

The same information applies to the audio content. The lower the quality, the less bitrate is needed, and as the codec increases we can add surround sound audio to our Blu-ray disk in the form of a Dolby AC3 5.1 audio file. The beauty of audio is that the file sizes are a lot smaller than video, so sometimes a low quality video can be saved by using a high quality audio codec, such as WAV 48k uncompressed, if the video codec allows for it.

Spend the time necessary to investigate the many Render As options available to you in Sony Vegas Pro 11 and your knowledge of the video editing world will begin to expand more than you ever thought possible.

Summary

In this chapter we covered a lot of information dealing with the finalizing of a project and creating a master file to deliver our project. We discussed:

- Video and audio compression and why the need for it
- Codecs that apply to video and audio renders and their differences
- How to use this knowledge to create master files to use in DVD Architect authoring software
- Considerations for creating video for the Web
- Burning a single movie disc from the timeline
- We also discussed other considerations when selecting your Render As settings in Sony Vegas Pro 11

The knowledge you have now acquired will de-mystify the process of video editing and the creation of DVD and Blu-ray files for you. Once again I would highly recommend going over this chapter a few times to ensure you haven't missed any points, and that you have the best understanding of the processes.

I would like to wish you all the best in your future video productions using Sony Vegas Pro 11.

Pop Quiz Answers

Chapter 2, Let the Magic Begin: Beginning the Project and Acquiring Media

Which of the following Project Properties would be incorrect if my Video was to be burned to a PAL DVD Disk	Correct answer is D. Ans=> Frame rate of 24.000 frames per second

Chapter 3, Video Editing Concepts and Application

To make an Edit or Split point to a media clip, we use the key combination?	Correct answer is D Ans=> The "S" key on it's own
To remove an unwanted piece of a media clip that has been cut from the timeline we use?	Correct answer is both A and B Ans=> Ctrl + X and The Delete Key
Which tool has to be enabled to have all three Takes visible on your preview monitor at the same time?	Correct answer is C Ans=> The Enable Multicamera Editing Tool
In Vegas Pro 11, zooming in on a subject in a scene is done by using?	Correct answer is C Ans=> The Event Pan/Crop Tool
Slow Motion or slowmo is achieved by?	Correct answer is C Ans=> Using the Smart tool while holding down the Ctrl key

Chapter 8, The Importance of Audio

Which of the 3 pre inserted plug-ins on the Audio Track FX is best used to get rid of High Frequencies from an Audio Clip?	Correct answer is C Ans=> The Track EQ
If the Ratio of a Track Compressor is set to 10:1, and the level increases 20 dB above the threshold, what would the increased volume at the output be?	Correct answer is B Ans=> 2dB

Chapter 10, Can I Put This On YouTube?: Rendering and Delivering the Final Project

The word codec is derived from which two words?	Correct answer is C Ans=> Compression Decompression
Of the many audio formats available, which one is currently the format of choice for audio CDs?	Correct answer is D Ans=> Wave
When preparing video and audio files to be used in Sony DVD Architect, which of the following is the correct method?	Correct answer is D Ans=> All of the above

Index

subtractive EQ 185
supplied clips
   used, for setting Project Properties 34, 35
Surround Panner window 216
Surround sound concepts 214, 215
Surround Sound Mixer 214
Surround Sound tools
   accessing 215
   Master Bus window 215
   Surround Panner window 216
   using 216, 217

T

Third Generation Partnership Project 222
title
   animating 109-114
Titler Collections 117
titles and text
   opening or closing titles, creating 114
Tones clip 180
tones file
   loading and listening 177-179
Track 3 82
Track Compressor plugin. *See* Compressor
      plugin 180
Track EQ 218
Track EQ plugin 180
Track FX plugin 180
Track Motion tool
   about 162
   two tracks, moving together 162-167
Track Noise Gate plugin 189
Transition
   Cross Effect transition 92
   features 93
   using 91, 92, 93
Transitions
   about 118
   effective transitions, creating 118-123, 124
Transitions window 19
Trimmer window 15

U

unwanted shadow
   removing, Pan / Crop tool used 72, 73

User Interface
   customizing 23-26

V

Vectorscope
   about 141
   using 141, 143
Vegas Pro 11
   Audio 101 176
   audio, concepts 176
   audio formats 225
   color correction techniques 127
   cropping tool 46
   editing tools 81
   Event Pan/Crop tool 49
   Fade Offset tool 47
   Keyboard Shortcuts 53
   media clips, splitting or cutting 48
   Multicamera tool 63
   music copyright 212
   Opacity tool 47
   pan/crop automation process 151
   pan/crop tool, automating 152
   parameter automation 157
   Preview monitor 37, 38
   project, creating 30
   Project Properties window 30
   smart tool 46
   spoken word, recording 202
   surround sound concepts 214
   Surround Sound tools, using 215
   titler tools 101
   titles and text 101
   Track Motion tool 162
   Transitions 118
   video compression 220
   video, editing 55, 56
   voice over, recording 206
Vegas Pro 11 Media
   Aspect Ratio 28
   overview 26
   PAL 28
   Video Formats 27
Vegas Pro 11 windows
   Device Explorer 22
   Explorer window 12

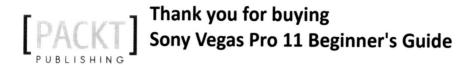

Thank you for buying
Sony Vegas Pro 11 Beginner's Guide

About Packt Publishing

Packt, pronounced 'packed', published its first book "Mastering phpMyAdmin for Effective MySQL Management" in April 2004 and subsequently continued to specialize in publishing highly focused books on specific technologies and solutions.

Our books and publications share the experiences of your fellow IT professionals in adapting and customizing today's systems, applications, and frameworks. Our solution-based books give you the knowledge and power to customize the software and technologies you're using to get the job done. Packt books are more specific and less general than the IT books you have seen in the past. Our unique business model allows us to bring you more focused information, giving you more of what you need to know, and less of what you don't.

Packt is a modern, yet unique publishing company, which focuses on producing quality, cutting-edge books for communities of developers, administrators, and newbies alike. For more information, please visit our website: www.PacktPub.com.

Writing for Packt

We welcome all inquiries from people who are interested in authoring. Book proposals should be sent to author@packtpub.com. If your book idea is still at an early stage and you would like to discuss it first before writing a formal book proposal, contact us; one of our commissioning editors will get in touch with you.

We're not just looking for published authors; if you have strong technical skills but no writing experience, our experienced editors can help you develop a writing career, or simply get some additional reward for your expertise.

Cinema 4D R13 Cookbook

ISBN: 978-1-849691-86-4   Paperback:514 pages

Elevate your art to the fourth dimension with Cinema 4D

1. Master all the important aspects of Cinema 4D

2. Learn how real-world knowledge of cameras and lighting translates onto a 3D canvas

3. Learn Advanced features like Mograph, Xpresso, and Dynamics.

4. Become an advanced Cinema 4D user with concise and effective recipes

Learning Adobe Edge

ISBN: 978-1-849692-42-7   Paperback: 300 pages

Create engaging motion and rich interactivity with Adobe Edge

1. Master the Edge interface and unleash your creativity through standard HTML, CSS, and JavaScript

2. Packed with an abundance of information regarding the Edge application and related toolsets

3. Robust motion and interactivity through web standards

3. Those approaching Edge from Adobe Flash Professional will find many references and tips for a smooth transition